The Greenpeace Guide to Anti-environmental Organizations

Carl Deal

Odonian Press
Berkeley, California

Additional copies of this book and others in the Real Story series are available for $5 + $2 shipping per *order* (not per book) from Odonian Press, Box 7776, Berkeley CA 94707. To order by credit card, or for information on quantity discounts, please call us at 800 REAL STORY, or 510 524 4000. Distribution to book stores and book wholesalers is through Publishers Group West, Box 8843, Emeryville CA 94662, 510 658 3453 (toll-free: 800 788 3123).

───────────

Odonian Press gets its name from Ursula Le Guin's wonderful novel *The Dispossessed* (though we have no connection with Ms. Le Guin or any of her publishers). The last story in her collection *The Wind's Twelve Quarters* also features the Odonians.

Odonian Press donates at least 10% (last year it was 36%) of its aftertax income to organizations working for social justice.

───────────

Greenpeace, USA.
    The Greenpeace guide to anti-environmental organizations/
Greenpeace: Carl Deal.
        p. cm. —(Real story series)
    Includes bibliographical references and index.
    ISBN 1-878825-05-4 : $5.00
    1. Green movements—United States. 2. Environmental policy—
United States. 3. Pressure groups—United States—Directories.
I. Deal, Carl. II. Title. III. Series.
JA75.8.G77   1993
324'.4'02573—dc20   92–46096
                                                         CIP

───────────

Printed in the United States of America   First printing: April, 1993

Acknowledgements

I am grateful to Martha Honey for lending her creativity and expertise, as both a journalist and a political activist, to this project. This book is her brain-child. Also, as this book expands upon the work of many other activists, journalists and researchers, I want to particularly thank Colleen McCrory, David Orr, and Connie Stewart. I also owe a word of thanks to Tia Lessin and to Greenpeace's Blair Palese, Meg Ruby, Cynthia Rust, Bill Walker, and Tamara Stark for their help with research and editing.

Credits

Main editor: Arthur Naiman

Developmental editor: Martha Honey

Line editors: Susan McCallister, Joan Baranow

Inside design: Karen Faria, Arthur Naiman

*Page layout, cover layout
    and production coordination: Karen Faria*

Basic cover design: Studio Silicon

Index: Steve Rath, Susan McCallister

Series editor: Arthur Naiman

Series coordinator: Susan McCallister

*Printing: Michelle Selby, Jim Puzey /
    Consolidated Printers, Berkeley, California*

Contents

Introduction

Until recently, environmental activists weren't taken very seriously. But after decades of battling industry and government bureaucracies to keep our air and water clean, to protect plant and animal species, to preserve the earth's atmosphere and to conserve natural resources, environmentalism has finally become a mainstream cause. The vast majority of people in the US and Canada now consider themselves environmentalists.

Predictably, this success has brought a backlash. With support from polluting industries and the far right, anti-environmental groups have declared war on every issue environmentalists support. Under the banner of free enterprise, democracy and economic growth, they advocate nuclear power, fossil-fuel development, expanding landfills, mineral exploration in national parks, private and commercial development of wetlands, and the repeal of crucial environmental legislation.

While many openly admit to being anti-environmental, most work in less visible ways. Ironically, at the same time they're attacking environmentalists in the media, courts and legislatures, they try to convince the public that they too care about the environment.

This book is designed to help you identify and understand these organizations. It gives you an overview of their ideologies, strategies and tactics, and tells you where their money comes from.

So don't be fooled by a green facade—look them up here first.

Chapter One

The anti-environmental movement

"Green on the outside, red on the inside—like a watermelon." That's how many anti-environmentalists characterize the environmental movement. As a former California forestry official warned a crowd of loggers and their families in 1991, "all environmentalists embrace some form of left-wing radical collectivism....As a result, today the greatest threat to you, to me, to our communities, to our state and to our nation, is no longer communism, it's not drugs, not AIDS, not crime, not poverty, not even liberal Democrats, but radical Environmentalism."

To fight this threat, many anti-environmentalists have developed deceptive jargon like *wise use, integrated resource management, sustainable development* and *multiple use.* They appeal to nationalistic pride, employ crude stereotypes, spread disinformation and even resort to physical violence.

Taken at face value, the claim that industrial growth can be balanced with the needs of nature has some merit. But *balance* is a word the anti-environmentalists merely mouth.

One of their favorite gambits is to say that environmental regulations cost jobs, when just the opposite is usually true. While some environmental laws may affect micro-regions, jobs are gained in areas like the development of new, cleaner technologies and alternative fuels, waste cleanups, etc.

Long before the Northern Spotted Owl was protected by the Endangered Species Act, timber jobs were falling prey to changes within the industry. While the volume of timber cut and processed in the US increased during the 1980s, the number of jobs declined, because companies adopted automated technologies and exported raw logs for processing abroad. (In 1988 alone, US companies exported over nine billion dollars worth of wood products for processing in Japan and Europe.) Environmentalists predict that an export ban would actually create 8000 jobs in the Pacific Northwest, without loosening environmental standards.

The same is true for other industries as well. Environmental regulations almost always create more jobs than they eliminate.

Greenwashing

According to a 1989 poll conducted by the Michael Peters Group, 89% of Americans are concerned with how products affect the environment, and 78% would pay more for a product packaged with recyclable or biodegradable materials. (These numbers would be, if anything, higher today.) By 1995, sales of "green" consumer products are expected to increase five times over their 1989 level.

As a result, businesses are wooing consumers by presenting themselves as environmentally responsible. All too often, however, this "green advertising" is based on half-truths and outright lies.

For example, Mobil Chemical added a small amount of starch to the plastic in their Hefty trash bags and began calling them "biodegradable." Unfortunately, this "biodegradability" only took place if the bags were left out in the sun, *not* if they were buried in landfills—which is, of course, where almost all garbage bags end up. And even in the unlikely event that one of these bags *was* left out in the sun, it wouldn't really biodegrade, but would merely break up into smaller pieces of plastic.

A Mobil Chemical spokesman later admitted that "degradability is just a marketing tool. We're talking out of both sides of our mouth because we want to sell our bags." The company was sued by six states and the Federal Trade Commission for making false and misleading claims, and Greenpeace issued a report written by Barry Commoner called *Biodegradable Plastics Scam*. Shortly thereafter, Mobil removed the word "biodegradable" from their packaging and agreed to stop making further unsubstantiated advertising claims.

The Coors Brewing Company sponsors a greenwashing campaign (called Pure Water 2000) that funds "grassroots organizations [engaged in] river cleanups, water habitat improvements, water quality monitoring, wetland protection and pollution prevention."

But in 1992, Coors pleaded guilty to charges that it had dumped carcinogenic chemicals into a local waterway for eighteen years. The company paid $750,000 in fines and now faces a $1,000,000 EPA lawsuit.

Corporations both at home and abroad brag that an era of "green business" has begun. At the 1992 Earth Summit, for example, 48 international business executives praised their Business Council for Sustainable Development (BCSD) for being on the cutting edge of corporate environmentalism. Meanwhile, they were maneuvering behind the scenes to minimize intergovernmental "meddling" in corporate affairs and to undermine key international treaties.

In both the US and Canada, corporations have pitted workers and labor unions against environmentalists, even while refusing to protect workers against economic hard times and technological change. The proposed North American Free Trade Agreement (NAFTA) between the US, Canada and Mexico now invites transnational corporations to exploit unprotected markets, cheap labor and raw materials abroad.

Grassroots organizing

Learning from the success of the environmental movement, anti-environmental corporate executives have launched their own grassroots campaigns. Organizations like Share B.C., People for the West! and the Yellow Ribbon Coalition stage local protests, organize letter-writing campaigns, hold media workshops, and canvass door-to-door.

But that's where similarities end. Most anti-environmentalists are heavily financed by industry and distort facts to manipulate public opinion. Many of them launch personal attacks against environmental activists and label them "anti-Christian," "anti-family" and "anti-American." They create false choices for the public by pitting jobs, family values and the economy against environmental concerns. And while environmentalists believe that we have a responsibility to safeguard nature and live in harmony with it, anti-environmentalists believe that we should dominate and exploit it.

Physical violence

Nonviolent organizations like Greenpeace and Earth First! have been branded as "terrorist" and subjected to surveillance and harassment by the FBI and other law-enforcement agencies, assaults, break-ins, arrests, sabotage and death threats. For example, in 1991, Greenpeace research scientist Pat Costner found her Arkansas home burned to the ground, along with twenty years of research on hazardous waste disposal. No one was ever arrested in connection with this crime.

In 1990, Earth First! organizers Judi Bari and Darryl Cherney were nearly killed when a bomb exploded in their car in Oakland, California. The FBI and local authorities responded to this event by arresting *Bari and Cherney!* They were accused of transporting a bomb that accidentally blew up, but the charges were soon dropped for lack of evidence. At least partially as a result of this ridiculous false start, the actual bombers were never apprehended.

In 1992, Stephanie McGuire of Perry, Florida, was assaulted by three men for opposing a local Procter & Gamble pulp mill that was dumping toxic waste into the Fenholloway River (it still is). They beat her, burned her with a lit cigar, cut her with a straight razor and taunted her by saying, "now you have something to sue us over." No one was ever arrested for this crime either.

These aren't isolated incidents. The Center for Investigative Reporting documented 104 violent attacks on environmentalists between January 1989 and January 1993—an average of one every couple of weeks—and it's investigating hundreds more.

The role of government

During the early 1980s, both the US and Canada moved far to the right. US Interior Secretary James Watt opened protected public lands, wildlife refuges and national parks to logging, mining and oil exploration. This made him one of the most unpopular cabinet officials ever, but Watt's legacy lives on.

Although George Bush called himself "the environmental president," his administration scrupulously safeguarded big business interests and ignored, vetoed or gutted environmental protection measures. For example, in 1992, he announced a moratorium on environmental regulations that lasted for eight months. Presented as a way to cut government spending, this election-year ploy undermined the Endangered Species Act (ESA)—which Bush once called "a sword aimed at jobs, families and communities"— the Clean Air Act and bans against logging on public lands.

The now-disbanded President's Council on Competitiveness, chaired by Vice President Dan Quayle, became corporate America's strongest ally on Capitol Hill. Corporations fighting regulation frequently found that a trip to the back door of the White House yielded quicker and better results than years of lobbying Congress or litigating in court.

Internationally, Bush's environmental record was equally appalling. He opposed global efforts to prohibit dumping radioactive wastes at sea, weakened an Antarctic mining ban and blocked efforts to prohibit shipping toxic waste and chemicals from the northern industrialized nations to the southern developing nations. At the 1992 Earth Summit in Rio de Janeiro, he refused to sign the biodiversity treaty, gutted the global warming agreement and vowed to oppose all international initiatives that didn't support a market-based solution to the environmental crisis.

President Clinton has pledged to value the environment as much as the economy, and Vice President Al Gore has impressive environmental credentials. But during the past twelve years, anti-environmentalists have gained real political muscle and made significant inroads into government. Under pressure from their lobbyists, Congress's environmental voting record has steadily declined since 1988.

Sixty percent of the judges currently sitting in the federal courts were appointed by Reagan and Bush. The once-liberal Supreme Court has been transformed into a body dominated by conservatives opposed to environmental regulation. The US courts are more likely than ever before to find federal regulation of the environment unconstitutional. Recent court rulings have protected private property and business interests at the expense of the environment (not to mention public health and safety).

So the prognosis isn't as bright as we'd like. But powerful as the anti-environmental movement is, it's ultimately doomed, because it doesn't have the truth on its side.

Chapter Two

Six types of anti-environmental groups

Some anti-environmental groups have a single focus, while others are multi-issue. Some are explicit about their mission, others cloak their agenda behind green rhetoric and still others are highly secretive about their activities. But for all their variety, they can be divided into six basic categories:

Public relations firms

Greenwashing has been a financial boon for major PR (public relations) firms. Transnational corporations themselves, they've often been hired to put clean faces on dirty industries and governments.

Headquartered in New York City, Burson-Marstellar (B-M) has 56 branches in 28 countries. During Argentina's "Dirty War" in the late 1970s, when the military dictatorship killed and "disappeared" thousands of political dissidents, B-M was brought in to sanitize the country's image and to attract foreign investment.

The firm also handled PR for Rumanian dictator Nicolae Ceausecescu and for the South Korean government during the 1988 Olympics in Seoul. B-M was retained to greenwash Exxon in the aftermath of the Valdez oil spill in Alaska and Union Carbide following the gas-leak disaster in Bhopal,

India. The Canadian timber industry is another client.

With 62 offices in 23 countries (its headquarters are in New York), Hill & Knowlton (HK) is another major PR firm involved in greenwashing oil, mining, waste management and other polluting companies.

But foremost in the greenwashing field is the Washington D.C.-based E. Bruce Harrison Co, which has been exclusively devoted to environmental PR for two decades. In 1990, *inside PR,* a national trade magazine, selected Harrison as the best in "environmental communication" for its success in solving problems for clients like Coors, the Chemical Manufacturers Association, Waste Management, Monsanto (asbestos) and the Motor Vehicle Manufacturers Association.

Corporate front groups

Many anti-environmental organizations are little more than corporate greenwashing campaigns created by high-priced PR firms and bankrolled by the corporations they represent. For example, in British Columbia, the B.C. Forest Alliance poses as a grassroots movement seeking forest preservation. But, as the *Vancouver Sun* revealed, the Canadian timber industry paid Burson-Marstellar one million dollars to create the Alliance.

Like its US counterparts—The Evergreen Foundation and the National Wetlands Coalition—the Alliance has two tasks: convincing the public that the current rate of environmental destruction can be maintained or increased without long-term effect, and persuading lawmakers to roll back unprofitable environmental regulations.

Think tanks

While industry greenwashes its image, right-wing think tanks like the Heritage Foundation and the Cato Institute often whitewash environmental crises, claiming they don't really exist. They've now been joined by groups like Citizens for the Environment and the Science and Environmental Policy Project, whose entire focus is thwarting the environmental movement.

Legal foundations

Created and funded by big business, anti-environmental "public-interest" legal foundations like the Mountain States Legal Foundation, the Pacific Legal Foundation and the National Legal Center for the Public Interest use the courts to fight government regulations and citizen lawsuits aimed at protecting the environment. Tax-exempt (even though they're strong advocates for corporate interests), they're the right-wing equivalents of the American Civil Liberties Union, the Sierra Club Legal Defense Fund, the Center for Constitutional Rights and Canada's Law Union and Legal Aid Societies.

Tulane University professor Oliver Houck made an extensive study of nine of these foundations. He found that one of them, the Mountain States Legal Foundation (MSLF), took positions in at least 24 of its cases that "directly benefitted corporations represented on its board of directors, clients of firms represented in its board of litigation or major contributors to MSLF's budget." This was a trend in every legal foundation he studied. For example, Houck concluded that the Pacific Legal Foundation violated the IRS's primary regulations for public-interest law by representing the interests of its corporate backers in more than 50% of its cases.

In June 1992, right-wing legal foundations won a major Supreme Court victory that will seriously undermine attempts to extend environmental protection to private property. In Lucas v. South Carolina Coastal Commission, the court agreed that the government's regulation of a developer's private property was a government seizure, prohibited by the Fifth Amendment. Anti-environmental groups are using this case, and others like it, to argue that environmental protection is unconstitutional.

Endowments and charities

Ultra-conservative philanthropies and private endowments collaborate with industry to underwrite anti-environmentalists. In 1991 alone, four of the largest of these charities—the Lilly Endowment, the Carthage Foundation, the John Olin Foundation and the Sarah Scaife Foundation—collectively disbursed in excess of $150 million to right-wing think tanks, legal foundations, corporate front groups and other anti-environmental organizations. Acting essentially as conduits for corporate money, the Lilly Endowment disburses the fortune of pharmaceutical giant Eli Lilly, while Carthage and Scaife are part of the Pittsburgh-based Mellon steel empire.

Wise Use and Share groups

The Wise Use movement is a coalition of local anti-environmental organizations based mainly in the western US. It's funded by timber, mining, ranching, chemical and recreation companies and by their trade associations. The movement's founder, Ron Arnold, describes himself as a former environmentalist who has "seen the light." What light has he seen? Well, as he puts it, "we want to be able to exploit the environment for private gain, absolutely." (The Canadian equivalent of the Wise Use movement, the Share movement, is discussed below.)

As a consultant to US and Canadian timber companies, Arnold advises them to contribute to a Wise Use or Share group because "it can do things the industry can't. It can stress the sanctity of the family, the virtue of the close-knit community. And it can turn the public against your enemies." Wise Use activists are recruited from the ranks of workers at company meetings (which are often compulsory) and by door-to-door canvassers who claim that environmentalism is causing unemployment.

Arnold also runs the Center for the Defense of Free Enterprise and is the president of the Washington state chapter of the American Freedom Coalition (AFC), a political front for Rev.

Sun Myung Moon's Unification Church. (Moon's cult became notorious in the 1970s for its mass marriages and mind-control programming of members, and in the 1980s for its support of right-wing Latin American death squads.)

The AFC provided seed money for the 1988 conference in Reno, Nevada, that founded the Wise Use coalition. Hundreds of real estate developers, right-wing activists and representatives of off-road vehicle manufacturers and timber and mining companies entered into a pact "to destroy" their enemy—the environmental movement. They agreed on 25 goals. To give you a feeling for them, I've summarized nine of these goals below:

- "immediate development of the petroleum resources of the Arctic National Wildlife Refuge in Alaska"
- converting "all decaying and oxygen-using forest growth on the National Forests into young stands of oxygen-producing carbon-dioxide-absorbing trees to...prevent the greenhouse effect"
- opening "all public lands, including wilderness areas and national parks," to mineral and energy exploration, as well as to recreational vehicles
- exempting from the Endangered Species Act any species whose protection would interfere with resource exploitation
- opening 70 million acres of wilderness, currently protected by the Wilderness Act, to limited commercial development and recreational use

- logging 3.4 million acres of the Tongass National Forest in Alaska
- passing laws that would require environmentalists who want to bring court cases or administrative appeals against logging, mining or grazing plans to "post bonds equivalent to the economic benefit to be derived from the challenged harvest, plus cost over-runs," and to pay all costs if the industry prevails
- granting anti-environmental groups the right to sue environmentalists on behalf of industry
- implementing free-trade agreements that will allow US industry access to natural resources globally

Canada's Share movement mirrors the Wise Use movement (and, in fact, representatives of the Canadian timber industry attended the 1988 Wise Use Conference in Reno). A report by the Parliamentary Library of the Canadian House of Commons condemns the timber industry for using Share groups as lobbyists, concluding that their objective has been to "pit labour against environmentalists [and] to divide communities and create animosity in the very places where honest communication and consensus should be encouraged."

A former organic farmer and diesel mechanic named Patrick Armstrong is widely credited with building the Share Movement. Like Wise Use's Ron Arnold, he describes himself as a former environmentalist who switched sides.

Armstrong's clash with the environmental movement began when the provincial government of British Columbia decided to create a national park on part of Queen Charlotte's Island. He lost his battle against the park but gained public exposure, and was immediately called upon by MacMillan Bloedel and other Canadian timber companies to lead new Share campaigns. He now heads Moresby Consulting, a firm that advises the timber industry and other natural resource interests on how to use Share groups to battle environmentalists.

Chapter Three

A catalog of anti-environmental groups

Public relations firms, foundations, endowments and charities aren't listed separately, but are referred to where we cover the organizations they created or financed. Because of space limitations, the funding information included here is sometimes incomplete. In most cases, more detailed information is on file with the author and Greenpeace.

The Abundant Wildlife Society of North America (AWS)

12665 Hwy 59N
Gillette WY 82716
307 683 2826

The Abundant Wildlife Society was founded by former cattleman Dick Mader in 1989, to obstruct environmentalists' efforts to reintroduce the endangered grey wolf into Yellowstone National Park. AWS claims to have built a broad membership spanning all 50 states, Canada and Europe, but knowledgeable environmentalists call it a "minor irritation."

Dick's son Troy considers himself the world's leading expert on the wolf. In an effort to turn public opinion against wolves, he distributes booklets with gory photographs of deer, sheep and cattle allegedly mauled or killed by grey wolves. He claims that the reason "wolves regularly attack people in" India is that it "has a philosophy of environmentalism."

In the US, AWS has linked arms with the Wise Use movement and is a member of the Alliance for America. It's added the Endangered Species Act and other key environmental legislation to its hit list.

Funding

Members are primarily fur trappers, ranchers and hunters, but AWS doesn't publicly disclose their identities.

Officers

Dick Mader, President ♦ Troy Mader, Director of Research ♦ E.L. Leser, Public Relations

Accuracy in Media (AIM)

1275 K Street NW
Washington DC 20005
202 371 6710, fax: 202 371 9054

Accuracy in Media grew from a one-person crusade to a million-dollar-a-year operation by attacking the mainstream media for abandoning the principles of "fairness, balance and accuracy" in its reporting. New Right philanthropies, think tanks and media support its work, and many members of its advisory board are former diplomats, intelligence agents and corporate directors.

Chaired by Reed Irvine, AIM is linked to the Moonie cult via individual supporters and Rev. Moon's affiliates in Washington DC. Irvine's column appears regularly in Moon's *Washington Times* newspaper.

In the 1970s, Irvine endeared himself to the New Right by alleging that the corporate media was a propaganda tool for the Soviet

KGB and Fidel Castro. With the end of the Cold War, AIM now assails environmentalists as the "infiltrators" of the media establishment. (Yet a 1992 study of the three major networks and 33 major daily newspapers shows that environmental coverage has actually declined since 1990.)

Turner Broadcasting System drew Irvine's ire with a program called *One Child, One Voice*, part of the documentary series *Save the Earth* that aired before the Rio Earth Summit. In it, children from five countries discussed how problems like acid rain, global warming and the loss of biodiversity are affecting their homelands.

Irvine called the program a "cheap trick" that exploited the fears of children. It's no coincidence that many of AIM's strongest supporters are corporations that have helped create such problems—oil and gas companies, chemical manufacturers and so on.

Funding (partial list)
Bethlehem Steel ♦ Carthage Foundation ♦ Chevron ♦ Ciba-Geigy ♦ Coors Foundation ♦ Dresser Industries ♦ Exxon ♦ Lawrence Fertig Foundation ♦ Getty Oil ♦ Horizon Oil and Gas ♦ IBM ♦ Kaiser Aluminum & Chemical ♦ F.M. Kirby Foundation ♦ Mobil Foundation ♦ Pepsico ♦ Phillips Petroleum ♦ Smith Richardson Charitable Trust ♦ Texaco Philanthropic Foundation ♦ Union Carbide

Officers
Reed Irvine, Chairman ♦ Murray Baron, President ♦ Wilson C. Lucom, Vice President ♦ Donald Irvine, Executive Secretary ♦ Jon Basil Utley, Treasurer ♦ Milton Mitchell, General Counsel

Alaska "Support Industry" Alliance (ASIA)

4220 B St, Suite 200
Anchorage AK 99503
907 563 2226, 907 561 8870

Much of Alaska's North Slope (the state's coastal plain along the Arctic Ocean) has been drilled for oil, as have the waters of Prudhoe Bay. Environmentalists have managed to save only 10% of the North Slope—the Arctic National Wildlife Refuge (ANWR). But the oil industry wants that too, and in 1979, it launched the Alaska "Support Industry" Alliance (ASIA) to get it—even though the possibility of discovering significant oil reserves in the ANWR is slim.

The federal government estimates that even if oil were found in ANWR, it would most likely represent no more than 200 days' worth at the US's present rate of consumption. Needless to say, ASIA doesn't emphasize that fact in its slick advertisements, pamphlets, newsletters and videotapes.

Instead, it claims that lifting the restrictions on the ANWR would create 735,000 jobs in all fifty states. One widely placed newspaper ad shows a Gulf War veteran with the headline: "He put his life on the line, today he's in the unemployment line."

Even if the Alliance's job estimates were accurate (which is highly unlikely), they don't bother to say how long those jobs would last. The oil industry as a whole promotes a boom-and-bust economy which provides little or no job security in a rapidly declining and environmentally unsustainable energy market.

Another Alliance ad reads: "Environmental Activists have promoted the romantic notion that the coastal plain is some kind of pristine and delicate Arctic Serengeti, It is not. The area is a flat, frozen wasteland for much of the year." In fact, the ANWR is the birthing ground for a herd of 180,000 caribou and also hosts polar bears, brown bears, wolves, musk oxen and millions of migratory birds.

Funding (partial list)
Alaska Forest Association ♦ Alaska Miners Association ♦ Alaska Oilfield Maintenance ♦ Parker Drilling ♦ Price Waterhouse ♦ Pacific Legal Foundation ♦ Petro Star ♦ Tesoro Petroleum

Officers
Lowell Humphrey (ComRim Systems), President ♦ James Udelhoven (Udelhoven Oilfield Systems), Vice President ♦ Sally Ann Carey (Crowley Maritime), Vice President ♦ David Haugen (Lynden), Vice President ♦ Mary Sheilds (Northwest Technical Services), Secretary ♦ Gordon Stevens (VECO Environmental & Professional), Treasurer

Alliance for America

Box 246, Sublimity OR 97385
503 769 7923, fax: 503 769 7923
also: Box 450, Canoga Lake NY 12032
518 835 6702, fax: 518 835 2527

The Alliance for America is a nationwide Wise Use and property rights coalition formed in 1991 to "put people back into the environmental equation." It claims over 500 member organizations in all fifty states, but the vast majority of them are trade associations connected with the timber, mining and cattle industries. Many Alliance leaders own or operate sawmills, or tree-falling, trucking or shipping companies.

In September 1992, the Alliance brought 400 loggers, miners and ranchers to Washington DC for its second annual Fly-In for Freedom. Every member of Congress was visited by an Alliance member laden with fact sheets that purported to show how the Endangered Species Act, wilderness preserves and wetlands protection are destroying jobs and family values. At a press conference, a little girl was put before the cameras to plead for the government to help her family so they could have Christmas again.

Alliance spokesperson Valerie Johnson—nicknamed the Velvet Hammer for her subtle yet powerful public speaking style—blames the environmental movement for the economic woes of her constituents. "There's been a small band of radicals trying to turn this country upside down," she told the 1992 Fly-In crowd. "The environmentalists are really our hardcore enemies."

Funding (partial list)

American Farm Bureau Federation ♦ American Freedom Coalition ♦ American Mining Congress ♦ American Motorcyclist Association ♦ American Petroleum Institute ♦ American Pulpwood Association ♦ Chemical Manufacturing Association ♦ Land Improvement Contractors of America ♦ Marigold Mining ♦ National Cattlemen's Association ♦

National Rifle Association ♦ National Trappers Association ♦ Rocky Mountain Oil and Gas Association

Officers

June Chrisle, President ♦ David Howard, Vice President ♦ Harry McIntosh, Vice President ♦ Rita Caley, Vice President ♦ Cheryl Johnson, Secretary ♦ Tom Hirons, Treasurer

Alliance for Environment and Resources (AER)

1311 I St, Suite 100
Sacramento CA 95814
916 444 6592, fax: 916 444 0170

The Alliance for Environment and Resources was formed in 1985 by the California Forestry Association (CFA) to put a citizens' face on the timber industry. (The CFA, which represents California's largest forest-products companies, lobbies state and federal governments for fewer logging restrictions on public and private lands, and works to clean up the industry's public image.)

AER is the umbrella organization for California Wise Use organizations, and is itself a member of the national Wise Use umbrella, the Alliance for America. AER groups frequently confront, threaten and harass environmentalists.

Of the more than 30 groups that have joined AER since 1985, perhaps the best-known are the Yellow Ribbon Coalition (which also has branches in Oregon and Washington) and the Shasta Alliance for Resources and Environment, which was formed by the Redding Chamber of Commerce to fight logging restrictions in the Shasta-Trinity and Six Rivers national forests.

One of the more confrontational organizations in AER is Mothers' Watch, a group of wives and mothers of timber workers. It sponsors boycotts of local businesses that support the environmental movement and is a strong presence at anti-environmentalist rallies. Mothers' Watch founder, Candy Boak, is frequently spotted videotaping environmental protesters, a counterintelligence tactic pioneered by the FBI during the civil rights and peace movements.

Funding
California Forestry Association

Officers
Kathy L. Kvarda, Director

Alliance for a Responsible CFC Policy

2111 Wilson Blvd, Suite 850
Arlington VA 22201
703 243 0344, 703 243 2874

In the early 1970s, scientists found evidence that when chlorofluorocarbons (CFCs)—widely used as coolants in refrigerators and air conditioners and as industrial solvents—are released into the atmosphere, they cause depletion of the ozone layer, which protects the earth from the sun's ultraviolet rays. (CFCs also contribute to global warming.)

The Alliance for a Responsible CFC Policy was founded in 1981 by more than 400 CFC manufacturers, distributors and other companies to influence government regulation of CFCs. The Alliance is operated by a lobbying and consulting firm called Alcalde, Rousselot and Fay.

Despite the "responsible" in its name, the Alliance's real goal is to slow down the timetable for phasing out CFCs. It has also won approval for the continued manufacturing of dangerous alternatives to CFCs like hydrochlorofluorocarbons (HCFCs) and hydrofluorocarbons (HFCs). HCFCs still cause ozone depletion—they simply do so at a slower rate than CFCs. And while HFC's don't deplete the ozone layer, they are potent greenhouse gases that contribute significantly to global warming.

"The CFC industry has a track record of stalling in the face of mounting evidence that CFCs destroy the ozone layer," cautions Carolyn Hartmann, a lawyer with US Public Interest Research Group. "For 20 years, DuPont and the CFC industry have vigorously fought against CFC regulations."

The Alliance's PR, media and lobbying work has succeeded in delaying a complete CFC phaseout until at least January 1996.

Funding (partial list)

ARCO Chemical ♦ AT&T ♦ Air Conditioning and Refrigeration Institute ♦ American Petroleum Institute ♦ Amoco Foam Products ♦ Carrier ♦ Chemical Manufacturers Association ♦ Dow Chemical ♦ E.I. Du Pont ♦ GTE ♦ General Electric ♦ Hill & Knowlton

♦ IBM ♦ Institute of Heating and Air Conditioning Industries ♦ Sara Lee ♦ Society of the Plastics Industry ♦ Texaco Chemical ♦ 3M ♦ W.R. Grace

Officers

James Wolf, Chairman ♦ Kevin J. Fay, Executive Director ♦ David Stirpe, Legal Counsel ♦ Beth Lewis, Membership Coordinator

American Freedom Coalition (AFC)

800 K St NW, Suite 830
Washington DC 20001
202 371 0303

The American Freedom Coalition is one of the principal political offshoots of Rev. Moon's Unification Church. It was founded in 1987 by Moon's lieutenant, Col. Hi Bo Pak, to organize a third political party in each state and, according to Pak, "make it so that no one can run for office in the United States without our permission."

The policies it endorses are decidedly anti-environmental, anti-feminist and homophobic. And contrary to the grassroots image it tries to project, AFC appears to have little if any popular support. As a political party, it doesn't appear on the ballot in any state.

AFC became known for challenging what it called the "persecution of Oliver North." Columns by far-right stalwarts Jeanne Kirkpatrick, Pat Buchanan and North himself regularly appear in the organization's publication, the *American Freedom Journal.*

AFC was a principal financial backer of the 1988 convention in Reno that founded the

Wise Use movement, and has organized dozens of other Wise Use conferences since then. In fact, the director of the AFC's Environmental Task Force, Merrill Sikorsky, claims that AFC spawned the Wise Use Movement. Sikorsky claims that oil drilling in the Arctic National Wildlife Refuge and offshore in California and North Carolina would make the US not only self-sufficient in oil, but also an oil exporter, despite the fact that five years of oil is the most that could be extracted from all potential US reserves.

Funding
AFC's yearly budget exceeds $1 million. The national office sends direct-mail funding pleas to a list of 300,000. Five million dollars in seed money was provided by the Unification Church.

Officers
Richard H. Ichord and Bob Wilson, Co-Chairmen ♦ Robert G. Grant, President ♦ Philip Sanchez, Vice President

Blue Ribbon Coalition (BRC)

Box 5449
Pocatello ID 83202
208 237 1557, fax: 208 237 1566,
electronic bulletin board: 208 237 5488

The Blue Ribbon Coalition represents off-road motorcyclists and timber, oil and mining companies who want unfettered access to public lands. Their motto is, *preserving our natural resources for the public instead of from the public.*

BRC lobbies legislators and state and federal land managers to block new wilderness designations and to open up existing wildlife preserves for public and private use. BRC's executive director, Clark Collins, was honored as the most successful legislative lobbyist at a Wise Use leadership conference in Reno in June 1992. In addition to preserving dirt bike trails, Collins has also organized support for the timber industry, and for oil exploration in the Arctic National Wildlife Refuge, cattle grazing rights on federal lands and modifying the Endangered Species Act.

Funding (partial list)

American Honda ♦ American Petroleum Institute ♦ American Suzuki ♦ Boise Cascade ♦ Cycle News ♦ International Snowmobile Industry Association ♦ Kawasaki ♦ Louisiana-Pacific ♦ Motorcycle Industry Council ♦ Potlatch ♦ Western States Petroleum Association ♦ Yamaha

Officers

Joani DuFourd, President ♦ Clark Collins, Executive Director ♦ Pat Harris, Treasurer ♦ John Butterfield, Treasurer

B.C. Forest Alliance

210-1100 Melville St.
Vancouver BC V6E 4A6 Canada
800 563 TREE, 604 685 7507, fax: 604 685 5373

By 1991, public opinion polls showed widespread mistrust of Canada's timber industry because of clear-cutting and pollution from mills, and the international community had begun to compare British

Columbia's deforestation with Brazil's. Thirteen of Canada's largest timber companies brought in the international public relations expert Burson-Marstellar to create the B.C. Forest Alliance as a "citizens'" lobby group to address these public concerns and to clean up the timber industry's image.

The Alliance sends out a monthly newsletter, produces television programs and organizes media tours of clear-cut logging sites, sawmills and pulp and paper factories. Although it insists it's a non-partisan citizen group and not a public-relations front, the founding timber companies provided a $1 million operating budget.

Of its 30 board members, 20 are CEOs, corporate directors or consultants for forest industry companies, and its offices are in the same downtown-Vancouver building as Burson-Marstellar, Weyerhauser of Canada, West Fraser Mills and Enso Forest Products.

The Alliance's message is clear-cut: the economic survival of British Columbia—and possibly all of Canada—depends upon a vigorous timber industry. A 1991 study by the Alliance, called the *Economic Impact Statement*, claims that one in five people in Vancouver owe their jobs to the forest industry, and that taxes in the entire province would increase $1,000 per person if the timber industry were restricted. Ironically, as critics like Jim Fulton (NDP–Ottowa) point out, forest companies themselves are eliminating thousands of timber jobs because of mechanization and increased exports.

Funding

Weldwood of Canada ♦ Doman Forest Products ♦ MacMillan Bloedel ♦ Canadian Forest Products ♦ Northwood Pulp and Timber ♦ Lignum ♦ West Fraser Timber ♦ Crestbrook Forest Industries ♦ Weyerhauser Canada ♦ Skeena Cellulose ♦ International Forest Products ♦ Riverside Forest Products ♦ Scott Paper ♦ Eurocan Pulp and Paper ♦ Fletcher Challenge Canada ♦ Canfor

Officers (partial list):

Jack Munro, Alliance Chairman ♦ Patrick Moore, Director, Forest Practices Committee ♦ Tom Buell (CEO, Weldwood of Canada) ♦ John Kerr (CEO, Lignum) ♦ Ray Smith (CEO, McMillan Bloedel)

Business Council for Sustainable Development (BCSD)

World Trade Center, Third Floor
Route de L'Aeroport 10
Geneva Switzerland
CASE Postale 365 CH 1215 Geneva 15
41 22 788 3202; fax: 41 22 788 3211

The 1992 Earth Summit in Rio was attended by leaders of 172 nations and hundreds of nongovernmental groups representing women, indigenous people, youth, farmers and environmentalists. But it was also exploited for "green" publicity by many of the transnational corporations responsible for creating the very problems the conference addressed. Represented by the Business Council for Sustainable Development, with the help of public relations giant Burson-Marstellar, these corporations played a key role in watering down treaties on biodiversity and global warming that were signed at the Earth Summit.

The BCSD was founded in 1991 by billionaire Swiss industrialist Stephen Schmidheiny, whose longtime friend and trusted advisor is Maurice Strong, a Canadian businessman who was the chief architect of the Earth Summit. So integral were the links between BCSD and the Earth Summit that a Burson-Marstellar consultant in New York referred to the Earth Summit as "the parent organization" of the BCSD.

The BCSD was hailed as marking a turning point towards responsible corporate behavior to protect the environment. But its philosophy, as outlined in *Changing Course*, a book it prepared for the Summit, has a familiar ring. It centers on economic growth through free trade, open markets, easy access to raw materials and voluntary corporate protection of the environment. After the Earth Summit, BCSD cut back its operations, keeping a small staff in Geneva and trying to decide, a spokesperson said, "if there is any post-Rio role for us."

Funding (partial list)
Chevron ♦ Volkswagen ♦ ConAgra ♦ 3M ♦ Ciba-Geigy ♦ Nissan Motor ♦ Nippon Steel ♦ Mitsubishi ♦ Dow Chemical ♦ Browning-Ferris Industries ♦ Royal Dutch Shell ♦ E.I. DuPont

Officers
Stephan Schmidheiny, Chairman ♦ James Hugh Faulkner, Executive Director ♦ David Harris, Executive Officer

California Desert Coalition (CDC)

6192 Magnolia Ave, Suite D
Riverside CA 92506
714 684 6509

The California Desert Coalition was formed in 1986 to fight Sen. Alan Cranston's (D–CA) California Desert Protection Act—now sponsored by Dianne Feinstein (D–CA)—which designates over seven million acres of desert as wilderness and national park. Under the Act, mining, off-road recreation and cattle grazing—which cause erosion, pollution and threaten desert species with extinction—would be virtually banned in about four million acres of proposed California wilderness area, and restricted in an additional 2½ million acres.

CDC says that 20,000 jobs are at stake if mining companies are forced to comply with these proposed regulations, and that the entire state economy would suffer if the law is passed. Such scare tactics have helped generate modest grassroots support. But, while it claims to be a voice for over a million Californians, CDC is really a front for mining companies, off-road vehicle trade groups and cattle ranchers.

Once the battle over desert preservation is settled, the Coalition is prepared to continue its crusade on behalf of the larger anti-environmentalist cause. Wise Use Movement leaders from the Center for the Defense of Free Enterprise (CDFE) were brought in to train CDC activists at the Second Annual

Desert Conference in May 1992. The CDC supporters were warned, "What is really behind the environmental movement is the largest scam of all time. What they are really after is to relieve people of their property."

Funding

According to Mike Ahrens, CDC media director, most financial support comes from individual members writing personal checks, with the larger companies and organizations "donating a little here and there—to help pay rent." The following corporations are represented on the steering committee: American Motorcyclist Association, District 37 ♦ High Desert Multiple Use Association ♦ Western States Public Lands Coalition ♦ Western States Petroleum Association ♦ High Desert Cattlemen's Association ♦ Western Mining Council ♦ California Off Road Vehicle Association ♦ Motorcycle Industry Council

Officers

Patrick Davidson, President ♦ David M. Hess, Chairman ♦ M.H. "Merv" Hemp, Editor, *Desert News Letter*

The Cato Institute

224 Second St SE
Washington DC 20003
202 546 0200, fax: 202 546 0728

This right-wing think tank, founded in 1977, sponsors policy conferences and distributes publications on issues as diverse as the global economy, military intervention and "ecoterrorism." Cato views the environmental movement and the demands it places on industry as a major obstacle to its vision of small government and an unregulated economy.

"The plain fact is that the gloom and doom about our environment is all wrong," Cato adjunct scholar and University of Maryland business professor Julian Simon told a 1992 policy conference. Cato's director of natural resource studies, Jerry Taylor, wrote in *USA Today* that "natural resources are better protected by individual owners with vested interests in their property" than by the government. "Environmental treaties are biased against economic growth despite the proven correlation between wealthy economies and healthy environments."

Funding (partial list)

American Farm Bureau Federation ◆ American Petroleum Institute ◆ Ameritech Foundation ◆ Amoco Foundation ◆ ARCO Foundation ◆ Association of International Auto Manufacturers ◆ Lynde and Harry Bradley Foundation ◆ Coca-Cola ◆ William H. Donner Foundation ◆ Exxon ◆ Ford Motor Company Fund ◆ JM Foundation ◆ Koch Industries ◆ Vernon K. Krieble Foundation ◆ Claude R. Lambe Foundation ◆ Liberty Fund ◆ Lilly Endowment ◆ Phillip M. McKenna Foundation ◆ Monsanto ◆ Motorola Foundation ◆ NBC ◆ Pfizer ◆ Philip Morris ◆ Procter & Gamble Fund ◆ Sarah Scaife Foundation ◆ Toyota Motor Sales

Officers (partial list)

William Niskanen, Chairman ◆ Edward H. Crane, President and CEO ◆ David Boaz, Executive Vice President ◆ Doug Bandow, Senior Fellow ◆ Robert J. Smith, Director Environmental Studies ◆ Jerry Taylor, Director of Natural Resource Studies

Center for the Defense of Free Enterprise (CDFE)

12500 NE 10th Pl
Bellevue WA 98005
206 455 5038

Founded in 1976 by Alan Gottlieb to champion conservative national policies, the Center for the Defense of Free Enterprise has evolved into the premier think tank and training center for the Wise Use movement. Through seminars, conferences, training videos, radio programs, books and newsletters, it teaches Wise Use activists in the US and Canada how to "fight back" against environmentalists. CDFE declares that environmentalists are not only inhumane "nature worshippers" but a national security risk whose goal is to destroy free enterprise.

The Center's outspoken director, Ron Arnold, proudly acknowledges that the ultimate goal of the Wise Use Movement is "to destroy" the environmental movement. "We're mad as hell, we're dead serious. We're going to destroy them," he told the *Portland Oregonian.* The Center has won support from more than a dozen conservatives in Congress and from Dick Cheney who was President Bush's Defense Secretary.

Although many New Right funders have supported the Center's work, Arnold and Gottlieb claim they don't rely on large corporate donations. Gottlieb is considered one of the most talented direct-mail fundraisers in the country, and reportedly sends out twenty million pieces of mail each year. This nets $5 million annually for CDFE and its sister organization, the Citizen Committee for the Right to Bear Arms. In 1984, Gottlieb spent a year in jail for filing false tax returns.

Funding (partial list of early supporters)

Coors Foundation ♦ Georgia Pacific ♦ Louisiana-Pacific ♦ MacMillan Bloedel ♦ Pacific Lumber ♦ Exxon ♦ DuPont, Agricultural Products Division ♦ Boise Cascade ♦ Seneca Sawmills ♦ Sun Studs ♦ Burkland Lumber ♦ F.M. Kirby Foundation

Officers

Alan M. Gottlieb, President ♦ Ron Arnold, Executive Vice President ♦ Samuel M. Slom, Vice President ♦ Merrill R. Jacobs, Secretary ♦ Jeffrey D. Kans, Treasurer

"Congressional Advisors (1992)" *(most have co-authored anti-environmental legislation)*

Senators Alfonse D'Amato (R–NY), Jesse Helms (R–NC), Don Nickles (R–OK), Ted Stevens (R–AK); Representatives Philip Crane (R–IL), Mickey Edwards (R–OK), Robert L. Livingston (R–LA), Don Young (R–AK); former Senator Gordon Humphrey (R–NH); former Representatives John Hiler (R–IN), Stan Parris (R–VA) Guy Vander Jagt (R–MI).

"Distinguished Advisors (1992)"

Dick Cheney, former US Secretary of Defense; Charles S. Cushman, National Inholders Association; Donald Devine; Bettina Bien Graves; Wayne Hage; Richard Ichord, American Freedom Coalition; Barbara Keating, Consumer Alert; Dawson Mathis; William Simon, Heritage Foundation

Citizens Coalition for Sustainable Development—see Share B.C.

Citizens for the Environment (CFE)

470 L'Enfant Plaza SW
Washington DC 20024
202 488 7255

Citizens for the Environment describes itself as a "grassroots environmental group that promotes market-based methods for protecting our environment." Despite this claim, it has no citizen membership of its own. Founded in 1990 as an offshoot of Citizens for a Sound Economy (a right-wing "consumer" group), CFE is a think tank and lobbying group that advocates strict deregulation of corporations as the solution to environmental problems.

It rallied opposition to the Clean Air Act of 1990 and to California's Proposition 128 ("Big Green"), a broad environmental package to improve state regulation of toxins. Congress passed the Clean Air Act, but Proposition 128 was defeated.

CFE scientist Jo Kwong urges the public to "discard the hype" circulated by environmentalists. She identifies sixteen environmental problems that she says are a sham. These "myths"—acid rain, natural-resource depletion and shrinking landfill space—"dictate public policy" Kwong complains.

CFE argues that industry has always played a positive role in protecting the environment. "The introduction of free-market economics—which occurred about the same time as the American Revolution—enabled us to grow wealthier, which in turn gave us the technology to grow healthier," CFE President Stephen Gold told an EPA conference. "Two centuries later, we've reduced and even eliminated many of our previous environmental threats." Gold concludes that natural resources will be preserved for future generations only "by channelling the powerful forces of the marketplace—that invisible hand—to enable this country to enter the next century cleaner and healthier than ever before."

Funding

CFE's parent, Citizens for a Sound Economy, is partially funded by:

Alcan Aluminum ♦ American Petroleum Institute ♦ Ameritech ♦ Amoco ♦ Association of International Automobile Manufacturers ♦ Boeing ♦ Chevron ♦ Coors ♦ General Electric ♦ General Motors ♦ Georgia-Pacific ♦ Honda North America ♦ Hyundai America ♦ Kobe Steel ♦ Mobil ♦ Nissan ♦ John M. Olin Foundation ♦ Phillip Morris ♦ Rockwell International ♦ Sarah Scaife Foundation ♦ Sony ♦ Toyota ♦ Union Carbide ♦ Xerox

Officers

Stephen Gold, President ♦ Michael Giberson, Senior Analyst ♦ Angela Logomasini, Senior Analyst

Citizens for Total Energy (CITE)

Box 563
Sunol CA 94586
510 862 2331

Citizens for Total Energy is a "grass roots energy education organization" run from the home of Helen Hubbard in a distant suburb of San Francisco. Hubbard founded CITE in 1977 to fight "anti-nuclear fanaticism" in California. "[O]ur efforts have been at convincing the general public and legislative bodies that the atom, in all its commercial applications, is not to be feared, but to be understood and that it is a friend to humanity, not an enemy," she says. "There are no other pro-nuclear grassroots organizations left. They all folded," laments Hubbard.

The US Council on Energy Awareness and other industry groups work very closely with CITE. In 1989, the American Nuclear Industry Council, nuclear power's largest trade association, presented Hubbard with a plaque and a cash prize for being the most effective pro-nuclear "grassroots" organizer.

Funding
Annual dues from individual members (CITE claims no financial relationship with industry).

Officers
Helen Hubbard, President ♦ Diane Hughes, Vice President ♦ Vada Ulrech, Secretary ♦ Kaliko Castaneda, Treasurer

Coalition for Vehicle Choice (CVC)

c/o E. Bruce Harrison & Co
1440 New York Ave NW
Washington DC 20005
800 AUTO 411

In 1991, E. Bruce Harrison & Co was paid $500,000 by the automobile industry to set up the Coalition for Vehicle Choice. With headlines like "Who should choose your next car? You or Congress?", this supposed consumer advocate and auto safety group launched an $8 million campaign that helped defeat a bill setting higher fuel-efficiency standards in US-built cars.

One of their TV commercials shows official crash-test footage of a compact car crumpling against a Ford Crown Victoria, the largest US-built passenger car. The voice-over warns, "The laws of physics cannot be legislated away." In fact, the safety features of the small car were sufficient to assure the survival of its driver.

"It is bitterly ironic that the auto industry has created an organization that purports to promote safer cars," said Joan Claybrook, president of the consumer group Public Citizen and a former administrator of National Highway Transportation Safety Administration (NHTSA). "Automobile companies have spent a fortune since the 1960s to oppose every single important safety measure that has ever been proposed."

The CVC campaign has been effective, thwarting fuel-efficiency increases in 1991 and 1992. But their scientific assertions are highly inaccurate and misleading. For example, they argue that increased fuel efficiency will have little or no effect on reducing air pollution or curbing global warming, even though automobile emissions are one of the largest contributors to both problems.

CVC President Diane Steed headed the NHTSA under Reagan, where she allied herself with the auto industry in fighting consumer groups and environmentalists. Steed herself lowered fuel-efficiency standards between 1986 and 1988.

Funding (partial list)

American Farm Bureau Federation ◆ American Motorcyclist Association ◆ Association of International Automobile Manufacturers ◆ International Snowmobile Association ◆ Livestock Marketing Association ◆ Motor Vehicle Manufacturers of America ◆ Motorcycle Industry Council ◆ National Automobile Dealers Association ◆ Recreation Vehicle Industry Association ◆ US Chamber of Commerce

Officers

Diane Steed, President ◆ Jeffrey B. Conley (of E. Bruce Harrison & Co), Executive Director

Committee for a Constructive Tomorrow (C-FACT)

Box 65722
Washington DC 20035
202 429 2737

Formed in 1985 to "protect our fragile environment" through public education and campus organizing, the Committee for a Constructive Tomorrow is a free-market think tank, corporate front group and citizen activist network, all rolled into one. With 2500 supporters and a $200,000 budget, its mission is to attack environmentalists and promote nuclear technology.

To solve waste management problems, C-FACT proposes creating new landfills and implementing voluntary—not mandatory—recycling programs. C-FACT also called for increased use of herbicides and pesticides, a rollback of federal air and water quality standards and a repeal of the Endangered Species Act.

C-FACT compares the leaders of the environmental movement to Hitler, Stalin and Genghis Khan: "Although garbed in Armani suits instead of battle armor and firing off press releases rather than artillery rounds, these ideologues are no less hungry for world predominance than their ruthless predecessors."

The Moonie-owned *Washington Times* newspaper regularly prints C-FACT views on global warming, acid rain and ozone depletion. C-FACT director Norval Carey is also the treasurer for the American Nuclear Energy Council and a registered lobbyist for General Atomics.

Funding (partial list)

Carthage Foundation ♦ US Council on Energy Awareness

Officers

David M. Rothbard, President ♦ Craig J. Rucker, Executive Director ♦ Sheryl Brinson, Director ♦ Norval E. Carey (Senior Vice President, General Atomics Corporation), Director ♦ Janet Raschella, Director ♦ Edward C. Krug, Director of Environmental Projects

Consumer Alert (CA)

1024 J St, Suite 425
Modesto CA 95354
209 524 1738

Consumer Alert is one of the most experienced mainstream anti-environmental groups. On the surface, it appears to be a consumer advocacy group like the

Public Interest Research Group (PIRG) or Ralph Nader's Public Citizen, but CA is actually backed by huge industry interests and is well-connected to the New Right. A 1990 study by two authentic consumer groups, Consumers Union and California PIRG, found that CA frequently takes positions that "tend to save industry money at the expense of consumer interests, such as safety, product testing, educational benefits and health."

Established in 1977, CA is dedicated to "the promotion of a free and open competitive marketplace, smaller government, lower taxes, free international trade and strong national economic growth." It unites Wise Use, industry front groups, right-wing think tanks and other anti-environmentalists in its thirty-six member National Consumer Coalition, which includes Accuracy in Media, Center for the Defense of Free Enterprise, Citizens for a Sound Economy, Committee for a Constructive Tomorrow, Heritage Foundation, Mountain States Legal Foundation, Pacific Legal Foundation, Reason Foundation, Science and Environmental Policy Project and Wilderness Impact Research Foundation.

After its 1990 Truth in the Environment conference, CA concluded that acid rain, global warming, pesticides and asbestos are having no serious impact on the environment or public health. CA's panel of scientists, including Ed Krug of Committee for a Constructive Tomorrow (C-FACT) and Fred Singer of the Science and Environmental Policy Project (SEPP), concluded that, under the greenhouse effect, "skin cancer would decline [and] many plants, including several agriculturally important species, would show enhanced growth."

Funding (partial list)

Anheuser-Busch ♦ Pfizer Pharmaceuticals ♦ Philip Morris ♦ Allstate Insurance Fund ♦ American Cyanamid ♦ Elanco ♦ Eli Lilly ♦ Exxon ♦ Monsanto Agricultural ♦ Upjohn ♦ Chemical Manufacturers Association ♦ AMR Foundation ♦ Ciba–Geigy ♦ The Beer Institute

Officers

Barbara Keating, President/Executive Director ♦ William C. McCleod, Chairman ♦ N. Richard Greenfield, Vice Chairman/Secretary ♦ Arthur Finkelstein, Treasurer

Defenders of Property Rights (DPR)

6235 33rd St NW
Washington DC 20015
202 686 4197

Defenders of Property Rights is a nonprofit legal foundation, founded in 1991 by husband and wife legal team Roger and Nancie Marzulla. It's the litigating arm of the property-rights movement and a member of the Environmental Conservation Organization (ECO). DPR fights in the courts to weaken regulations on wetlands, historic landmarks, environmental protection and land use.

Roger Marzulla is a former president of the Mountain States Legal Foundation and former assistant attorney general of the Environment and Natural Resources Division for the US Justice Department. Nancie Marzulla is also a veteran of the Mountain States Legal Foundation.

Funding

$250,000 annual budget

Officers

Nancie Marzulla, Director

Environmental Conservation Organization (ECO)

1300 Maybrook Dr
Maywood IL 60153
708 344 1556

The acronym *ECO* suggests an environmentally friendly agenda. In truth, the Environmental Conservation Organization was started in 1990 as a front group for real estate developers and other businesses opposed to wetlands regulations. It shares a suburban Chicago office with the Land Improvement Contractors of America, a national trade association for real estate developers.

ECO quickly grew into one of the broadest coalitions of anti-environmentalists in the US, claiming membership of seven million individuals and 320 organizations. The National Inholders Association, Defenders of Property Rights, the National Wetlands Coalition and National Rifle Association have joined the coalition. ECO believes that "efforts to save the environment should not erode fundamental constitutional rights nor pollute our free-enterprise economy."

Its 30-page monthly newsletter, *Eco-logic: People Balancing the Environmental Equation,* gives detailed updates on the progress of the Wise Use, Share and property rights movements. *Eco-logic* is distributed by other Wise Use and property rights groups and serves as a networking forum for their members.

In one issue, Sen. Steve Symms (R–ID) explains how his proposed Private Property Rights Act will mandate "no net loss of property" in place of "no net loss of wetlands," SEPP's Fred Singer discredits ozone depletion as "scientific ignorance" and NFLC's Jim Faulkner tells how to pass local laws to undercut federal environmental protection measures.

Funding (partial list)

Allnet Telecommunications ♦ Land Improvement Contractors of America ♦ American Farm Bureau Federation

Officers

Robert Vicks, Chairman ♦ Henry Lamb, Executive Vice President ♦ Rhonda McAtee, Director

The Evergreen Foundation

3979 Crater Lake Hwy
Medford OR 97504
503 779 4999

L ocated in the heart of Oregon's forest country, the Evergreen Foundation is a timber-industry front group that puts forth the idea, through films and videos, that forest resources are abundant. It paints itself as a friend to the environment and doesn't directly bash environmentalists. Its motto is *healthy environments and healthy economies go hand in hand.*

Its slick bi-monthly publication *Evergreen* has a circulation of 50,000 and looks more like a nature magazine than industry propaganda. Its pro-timber bias is carefully camouflaged by wildlife photographs and human-interest stories about fly-fishing. Evergreen's true message is that environmental protection laws are unreasonable, based on extreme views, founded in bad science and made without consideration of their social and economic impacts.

In its 1991–92 annual report, the Evergreen Foundation invites supporters to take a walk through the "Enlightened Forest," a world where "there is beauty, peace and mystery....people make decisions on the basis of what they know, not what they fear." There's nothing to worry about, because "we plant more than we harvest." In this nirvana, the only dangers to old growth forest are insects, fire and natural disaster; the only threat to the spotted owl is disease; and the only bad policies are those that reflect the "irrational" fears of environmentalists.

Funding (partial list)

The National Forest Products Association, the largest industry trade association, distributes Evergreen, but won't reveal its own funding or its relationship to the Evergreen Foundation. Other supporters include: MCI ♦ MasterCard ♦ Champion Paper

Officers

James D. Peterson, Executive Director ♦ Russell McKinley (Boise Cascade), Chairman of the Board ♦ Steve Carter (P&M Cedar Products), Vice Chairman ♦ Greg Miller (Southern Timber Industries Association), Treasurer

Foundation for Research on Economics and the Environment (FREE)

4900 25th NE, Suite 201
Seattle WA 98105
206 548 1776
also: 502 S 19th, #1
Bozeman MT 59715
406 585 1776

The Foundation for Research on Economics and the Environment is a think tank that advocates "resource development" in wilderness areas, national parks and other protected areas. Funded by New Right philanthropies and energy and natural resources industries, its annual operating budget has grown from $50,000 in 1986 to over $400,000. It convenes panels of scientists to refute ecological concerns and discredit environmentalists.

FREE uses language that makes it sound pro-environment. In 1987, FREE's chairman John Baden—who's also a member of the National Petroleum Council, an industry trade group—wrote in the *Wall Street Journal* that "exploration and development would work best under the aegis of private environmental groups." He points to the Audubon

Society's Rainey Sanctuary in Louisiana as an example of how business and environmental protection can coexist. "Natural gas wells have operated within the preserve for more than 25 years without measurable damage to the surrounding ecosystem."

However, for FREE, letting conservative environmental organizations manage wilderness areas is simply a way-station on the road to total privatization of federal lands. Under their plan, federal nature preserves like the Arctic National Wildlife Refuge (long coveted by the oil industry) would quickly be sold to the highest bidder.

Funding (partial list)
Amoco Foundation ♦ ARCO ♦ Carthage Foundation ♦ Donner Foundation ♦ Liberty Fund ♦ Murdoch Grant ♦ Noble Foundation ♦ Sarah Scaife Foundation ♦ Shell Oil Foundation

Officers
John A. Baden, President ♦ Jack Fay, Treasurer ♦ James Meigs, Vice President ♦ Richard Derham, Corporate Secretary

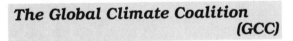

The Global Climate Coalition (GCC)

c/o US Chamber of Commerce
1615 H St NW
Washington DC 20062
202 463 5533, 202 775 0944

This front group was founded in 1989 by 46 corporations and trade associations representing "all major elements" of US industry. The mission of the Global Climate

Coalition is to convince Congress and the public that global warming is a myth. Executive Director John Shlaes, formerly a vice president with the Edison Electric Institute, claims that if global warming is taken seriously and carbon dioxide (CO_2) emissions are curbed, it will cripple "the nation's economy and the ability of the US to compete in international markets."

In 1992, GCC lobbyists helped weaken an energy bill presented in the House by George Miller (D–CA) which would have required sharp cutbacks in CO_2 emissions and banned virtually all new offshore oil and gas drilling for at least ten years. According to Rep. Miller, the GCC's only goal is the "unimpeded production of oil, gas and coal."

GCC also contributed to one of the greatest disappointments of the 1992 Rio Earth Summit. The International Panel on Climate Change (IPCC), a board of several hundred scientists from 40 countries, advised Earth Summit organizers that the only hope for avoiding unprecedented and ecologically disastrous global warming would be to make deep cuts in CO_2 emissions.

Throughout the two-year negotiating process leading up to the Summit, GCC aggressively opposed mandatory emissions controls; ultimately, their view prevailed. The final draft of the Convention supports only voluntary emissions controls and sets no timetable or targets for CO_2 reductions.

Funding

Coalition members include: ARCO ◆ American Electric Power Service Corp ◆ American Mining Congress ◆ American Petroleum Institute ◆ Amoco ◆ Association of American Railroads ◆ Association of International Automobile Manufacturers ◆ Chemical Manufacturers Association ◆ Dow ◆ DuPont ◆ Enron ◆ Kaiser Aluminum and Chemical ◆ Motor Vehicle Manufacturers Association ◆ National Coal Association ◆ Phillips Petroleum ◆ Texaco ◆ US Chamber of Commerce

Officers

John B. Shlaes, Executive Director ◆ Tia Armstrong (US Chamber of Commerce), Associate Manager/ Environmental Policy ◆ Glenn Kundert (US Chamber of Commerce)

The Heritage Foundation

214 Massachusetts Ave NE
Washington DC 20002
202 546 4400, fax: 202 544 6979

The Heritage Foundation was formed in 1973 by Joseph Coors, president of the Coors Brewing Company, who provided $250,000 seed money. By 1991, the Heritage Foundation had evolved into the pre-eminent conservative Washington policy center, promoting unrestricted free enterprise, anti-communism, deregulation of industry and a strong national defense based on an abundant nuclear arsenal. Its annual budget of over $19 million is funded by New Right endowments, automobile manufacturers, coal, oil and chemical companies, and many other large corporations.

Over the years, the Heritage staff and advisory board have included men tied to racist or neo-Nazi groups, the Unification Church and right-wing Christian fundamentalists. Despite this, Heritage was so influential with the Reagan Administration that an estimated two-thirds of its 1981 policy recommendations were adopted.

This included a proposal to open designated wildernesses to strip mining (drafted for Heritage by William Perry Pendley of the Mountain States Legal Foundation). Pendley was subsequently selected by Interior Secretary James Watt to formulate and implement federal mineral policy.

Heritage dismisses the environmental movement as "extremist." In one issue of its quarterly journal *Policy Review*, 39 leading conservatives presented a policy blueprint for the 1990s. They urged conservative activists to "[s]trangle the environmental movement," and called it "the greatest single threat to the American economy."

Policy Review editor Adam Meyerson added that "leading scientists have done major work disputing the current henny-pennyism about global warming, acid rain and other purported environmental catastrophes." Noting that "no organization is effectively bringing their arguments to public policy discourse," Meyerson suggested the establishment of a network of science and policy analysts to discredit the environmental movement. Since 1990, several "environmental" think tanks—including Citizens for the Environment and the Science and Environmental Policy Project—have joined Heritage in its attack on mainstream environmentalism.

Funding (partial list)

Alcoa Foundation ♦ Amoco Foundation ♦ Amway ♦ Boeing ♦ Lynde and Harry Bradley Foundation ♦ Carthage Foundation ♦ Chevron ♦ Coors Foundation ♦ Donner Foundation ♦ Dow Chemical ♦ Exxon ♦ Federation of Korean Industries ♦ Ford Motor Company Fund ♦ G.E. Foundation ♦ General Motors ♦ GTE ♦ IBM ♦ J.M. Foundation ♦ F.M. Kirby Foundation ♦ Eli Lilly ♦ Lockheed ♦ McKenna Foundation ♦ Mobil Oil ♦ Murdock Charitable Trust ♦ John M. Olin Foundation ♦ J. Howard Pew Freedom Trust ♦ Philip Morris ♦ Procter & Gamble Fund ♦ Pfizer ♦ Reader's Digest ♦ R.J. Reynolds Tobacco ♦ Sarah Scaife Foundation ♦ Shell Companies Foundation ♦ Texaco ♦ Union Pacific

Officers (partial list)

Dr. Edwin J. Feulner, Jr., President and CEO ♦ Phillip N. Truluck, Executive Vice President ♦ Burton Yale Pines, Senior Vice President ♦ John Von Kannon, Treasurer

Information Council for the Environment (ICE)

c/o Bracy Williams & Co
1000 Connecticut Ave NW
Washington DC 20036
800 346 6269, 202 659 4805

Established in 1991 as a front group for 24 coal companies, mining associations and public-utility corporations, the Information Council for the Environment is run by the Washington DC public relations firm of Bracy Williams & Co. As its acronym *ICE* implies, this group's goal is to persuade the government and public that global warming is a myth, and to thereby undermine conversion to less-polluting alternative energy sources, like solar, wind and hydroelectric.

(Fossil fuels like coal and oil release massive amounts of carbon dioxide when burned by industry and in automobiles, making them the largest single cause of global warming.)

ICE's greenwashing campaign warns that "any precipitous legislation in the US could spawn an economic disaster for the nation." After extensive market tests and polling, ICE decided to direct its advertising at older, "less-educated men," and low-income women— groups "not accustomed to taking political action." A test ad cast environmentalists as doomsday crazies: "Some say the earth is warming; some also said the earth is flat."

Funding (partial list)

AMAX Coal ♦ ARCO Coal ♦ Edison Electric Institute ♦ National Coal Association ♦ Ohio Valley Coal ♦ Peabody Holding Company ♦ Western Fuels Association ♦ Zeigler Coal Holding Company

Officers

Ivan Brandon, Executive Director ♦ Robert C. Balling, Jr., Science Advisor ♦ Sherwood B. Idso, Science Advisor ♦ Patrick Michaels, Science Advisor

The Institute for Justice (IFJ)

1001 Pennsylvania Ave NW, Suite 200 South
Washington DC 20004
202 457 4240, fax: 202 457 8574

Founded in 1991, the Institute for Justice is the newest addition to the ranks of conservative public-interest law firms. Business Week dubbed it the "ACLU of the right." One co-founder is Clint Bolik, who in years past was an aide to Clarence Thomas. The other is Chip Mellor, who was general counsel to the Energy Department under President Reagan.

IFJ clients are often small landowners and entrepreneurs, but their cases are carefully chosen to challenge laws and regulations that restrict free enterprise and protect the environment in any way. In Lucas v. South Carolina Coastal Commission, the Institute filed a friend-of-the-court brief urging the US Supreme Court to declare unconstitutional a state ruling protecting a fragile coastal ecosystem against a developer who wanted to build summer homes there. When the Supreme Court did so, an ecstatic IFJ immediately vowed to "employ this favorable case precedent in future challenges to government intrusions on the rights of property owners."

Funding (partial list)
Lynde and Harry Bradley Foundation ♦ Broyhill Family Foundation ♦ J.M. Foundation ♦ Koch Charitable Foundation ♦ John M. Olin Foundation ♦ Philip Morris ♦ Sarah Scaife Foundation

Officers

William H. (Chip) Mellor, President ♦ Clint Bolik, Vice President ♦ John E. Kramer, Director of Communications ♦ Steven J. Eagle, Senior Fellow

Keep America Beautiful (KAB)

9 West Broad St
Stamford CT 06902
203 323 8987

On the surface, it's the oldest and best-known US anti-litter campaign, but Keep America Beautiful is actually a sophisticated greenwashing operation. It's bankrolled (to the tune of $2 million annually) by some 200 companies that manufacture and distribute the aluminum cans, paper products, glass bottles and plastics that account for about a third of the material in US landfills.

Since the early 1970s, KAB has used over $550 million worth of donated advertising time and space to encourage guilty consumers to "put litter in its place" (coincidentally creating more business for KAB sponsors like Browning Ferris and Waste Management, who are ultimately paid to dispose of our trash). With videos, brochures, newsletters, school curricula, seminars and training workshops at its 460 local affiliates, KAB tells consumers that they're the ones responsible for this trash, and that they must solve the problem of litter by changing their habits.

Never does KAB call on industry to produce less, recycle more or set higher pollution standards. In fact, KAB President Roger Powers once assured a group of "grassroots" affiliates that "industry will fund you if you respond to its needs."

In line with many of its corporate backers, KAB opposes a national bottle bill that would reduce litter by requiring a five-cent deposit on all glass bottles. Recent, half-hearted support of recycling and composting programs doesn't change KAB's overall environmental record.

Funding (partial list)

3M ♦ Amoco Foam Products ♦ Bethlehem Steel ♦ Browning Ferris ♦ Anheuser-Busch ♦ ARCO Chemical ♦ Coca-Cola ♦ Dow Chemical ♦ E.I. Du Pont ♦ First Brands ♦ Georgia-Pacific ♦ McDonald's ♦ Mobil Chemical ♦ RJR Nabisco ♦ Scott Paper ♦ Seagram ♦ US Steel ♦ Waste Management

Officers and Executive Committee members
(partial list)

Roger W. Powers, President ♦ Donald Bolger (Mobil Chemical) ♦ James C. Bowling (Burson-Marstellar) ♦ David S. Buckner (Browning-Ferris) ♦ Philip J. Davis (Philip Morris) ♦ Kenneth M. Evans (Waste Management) ♦ Stephen K. Lambright (Anheuser-Busch) ♦ Charles L. Wosaba (Procter & Gamble)

Mothers' Watch—*see Alliance for Environment and Resources*

Mountain States Legal Foundation (MSLF)

1660 Lincoln St, Suite 2300
Denver CO 80264
303 861 0244, eco-terrorist hotline: 303 TESTIFY

"The environmental movement is the last refuge of the Left," says Mountain States Legal Foundation president William Perry Pendley, who served as an assistant secretary for energy and minerals in the Interior Department during the Reagan administration. "Because of the collapse of communism, because the wall has come down, because the Soviet Union is no more...the environmental movement is the last refuge of people who favor government over people."

Long before the fall of communism, MSLF was a leader in the anti-environmental movement. It was created in 1976 by the Coors Brewing Company and the National Legal Center for the Public Interest, with James Watt as its founding president.

Watt once invited corporate funders to meet directly with MSLF attorneys to develop a litigation strategy against a federal wilderness plan that would restrict their ability to develop resources on public lands. Such brazen collusion between big business and the non-profit sector was unprecedented then, but has since become customary.

MSLF's work on behalf of the rising New Right won it a reputation for being "anti-consumer, anti-feminist, anti-government, anti-

Black, and above all, anti-environmentalist."
When Watt was tapped by Reagan to be Interior Secretary, MSLF policy objectives were implemented nationally. Today, the MSLF remains at the core of the anti-environmental movement. Ron Arnold's Center for the Defense of Free Enterprise refers to MSLF as "the litigating arm of the Wise Use Movement."

Funding (partial list)

Amoco ♦ Chevron ♦ Coors Foundation ♦ El Pomar Foundation ♦ Exxon ♦ Ford ♦ Phillips Petroleum ♦ Texaco

Officers (partial list)

William Perry Pendley, President ♦ George M. Yates, Chairman ♦ Scott A. Crozier ♦ James McClure (former Idaho Senator) ♦ Dixie Lee Ray (former Governor of Washington) ♦ James R. Rothwell (Vice President, BHP Minerals) ♦ John Wilson (President, Pegasus Gold)

Multiple Use Land Alliance—see National Inholders Association

National Federal Lands Conference (NFLC)

Box 847
Bountiful UT 84011
801 298 0858

When Congress passed the National Environmental Policy Act (NEPA) in 1970, it intended to increase federal responsibility for land management by requiring an environmental impact study before any regulation or initiative could go into effect. They had no idea they were giving miners, ranchers and loggers a sword with which to fight environmental protection, but that's exactly what the National Federal Lands Conference is training them to do.

At NFLC conferences (sponsored by logging companies, ranchers, oil and gas companies and the like), lawyers specializing in property rights, Wise Use leaders like Ron Arnold and mining, ranching and timber executives teach rural communities how to subvert the Endangered Species Act and other federal statutes, which they say are eliminating jobs.

The hook they use is a NEPA provision that makes the federal government responsible for preserving "important historic, cultural and natural aspects of our national heritage." In the NFLC's pilot project, Catron County, New Mexico passed its own environmental laws which, it claimed, were in keeping with the town's "customs" and "heritage." NFLC claims that its lengthy legal battles have yielded a 95% success rate in overturning federal mining, ranching, logging and water use regulations in Catron County.

Funding

The NFLC claims to receive no membership dues, and chooses to keep the identity of its financial sponsors under wraps. The following corporations sponsored a 1992 NFLC conference in Eureka, California: MacMullin Forestry and Logging ♦ Redwood Coast Petroleum ♦ Louisiana-Pacific ♦ Redwood Region Logging Conference

Officers

Ruth Kaiser, Executive Director ♦ Jim Faulkner, Associate Director

National Inholders Association (NIA)

30218 NE 82nd Ave / Box 400
Battle Ground WA 98604
206 687 3087, fax: 206 687 2973, Multa-Net electronic bulletin board: 707 935 6170
also: 4 Library Court SE
Washington DC 20003
202 544 6156, fax: 202 544 6774

"**P**arks are like aspirin," quips Chuck Cushman, executive director of the National Inholders Association. "Two can be helpful, but a hundred will put you in the hospital." (An "inholder" is someone who owns land inside or along the boundaries of a national park or other protected area.)

Since founding the NIA in 1978, Cushman has become one of the most popular speakers on property rights and federal land use. His 16,000-member NIA is made up of property owners, mining companies, cattle corporations, timber firms and real estate developers who demand access to natural resources on public lands.

A leading strategy center for the Wise Use movement, NIA wants to open up federal and state-owned lands for development. "It's a holy war between fundamentally different religions," Cushman tells his audiences. "Preservationists are like a new religion—a new paganism. They worship trees and sacrifice people." Although Cushman claims to follow in the non-violent tradition of Ghandi and Martin Luther King, long-time activist Gary Ball of the Mendocino Environmental Center in Ukiah, CA says that "property destruction, arson, death threats" and other violence follow Cushman's appearances.

In 1988, Cushman set up MULTA (the Multiple Use Land Alliance), a coalition of Wise Use and property rights groups that offers NIA members training in high-tech political activities like running fax networks and electronic bulletin boards. NIA/MULTA has its own nationwide computer network, Multa-Net, which monitors new bills in Congress, roll-calls on recent votes, and information in the *Federal Register* and the *Congressional Record*.

Funding

NIA/MULTA doesn't publicly disclose its financial backers.

Officers

Charles S. Cushman, Executive Director ♦ Myron Ebell, Washington DC Representative ♦ Joseph T. Wrabek, Managing Editor, *National Inholders News* and *Multiple Use Advocate* ♦ Erich Veyhl, Chairman, Park Inholder Advisory Board ♦ Wayne Hage, Chairman, Grazing Advisory Board ♦ Don Fife, Chairman, Mining Advisory Board ♦ Paul Allman, Chairman, Recreation Residence Advisory Board

National Legal Center for the Public Interest (NLCPI)

1000 16th St NW, Suite 301
Washington DC 20036
202 296 1683

In the mid-1970s, a handful of corporate executives set out to create the ultimate right-wing legal foundation. They came up with the National Legal Center For the Public Interest, an umbrella organization that coordinates the activities of local legal foundations.

Founding president Leonard Therberg revealed the NLCPI position on environmental legislation in a planning memo leaked in 1975. "What we cannot accept," he wrote, "are mindless proposals that would sacrifice the people of the United States on an altar of nature." Executives from industrial-strength polluters like Coors, 3M and Dow Chemical, as well as arch-conservatives like *Washington Times* editor Arnaud de Borchaud and ex-CIA director William Webster, are on the NLCPI board of directors.

NLCPI member firms include the Mountain States Legal Foundation, Mid-America Legal Foundation, Gulf Coast and Great Plains Legal Foundation, Mid-Atlantic Legal Foundation, Southeastern Legal Foundation, New England Legal Foundation, Washington Legal Foundation and Capital Legal Foundation. Superfund, wetlands protection and wilderness protection have all fallen prey to these NLCPI firms.

Funding (partial list)

AT&T ♦ Bell Atlantic ♦ Bradley Foundation ♦ Coors Foundation ♦ Culpepper Foundation ♦ Exxon ♦ Ford Motor Company Fund ♦ Gulf Oil ♦ Hearst Foundation ♦ Kimberly-Clarke Foundation ♦ Mobil ♦ M.J. Murdock Charitable Trust ♦ John M. Olin Foundation ♦ Phillips Petroleum Foundation ♦ Sarah Scaife Foundation ♦ Texaco

Officers

Ernest B. Hueter, President ♦ Irene A. Jacoby, Vice President ♦ E. Donald Stumbaugh, Vice President and General Counsel ♦ N. David Thompson, Secretary ♦ Raymond P. Shafer, Treasurer

National Wetlands Coalition (NWC)

1050 Thomas Jefferson St NW, Seventh Floor
Washington DC 20007
202 298 1920, fax: 202 338 2146

E nvironmentalists have long fought to preserve wetlands—streams, ponds, lakes, swamps, marshes and coastal regions—because they're the habitat of one-third of all endangered species. (Wetlands also generate revenues of nearly $29 billion annually from sportfishing and hunting.)

In 1989, utility companies, miners and real estate developers hired the Washington law firm of Van Ness, Feldman and Curtis to lobby Congress to open wetlands to commercial development. They formed the National Wetlands Coalition and fund it with $40,000 annually.

The NWC lobbied former vice president Dan Quayle for a more restrictive definition of wetlands. Over protests by E.P.A. administrator William Reilly, President Bush accepted the definition proposed by Quayle's Council on Competitiveness, which effectively removed protection from nearly 50% of what had been called wetlands. Fortunately, the NWC definition was overturned by EPA head William Reilly during the transition from the Bush to the Clinton administration.

NWC also helped draft H.R. 1330, the Comprehensive Wetlands Conservation and Management Act, which proposes to restrict the definition of wetlands even further, and to have taxpayers compensate property owners (usually large corporations) for legal fees and financial losses when environmental restrictions are applied.

Funding (partial list)

American Mining Congress ◆ Amoco Production Co ◆ ARCO Alaska ◆ Arctic Slope Regional Corp ◆ Chevron ◆ Conoco ◆ Consolidated Natural Gas ◆ Enron ◆ Exxon ◆ Hunt Oil ◆ Kerr-McGee ◆ Marathon Oil ◆ Mobil Exploration & Producing ◆ Phillips Petroleum ◆ Shell Oil ◆ Texaco

Officers

H. Leighton Stewart (CEO of Louisiana Land and Exploration), Chairman ◆ Marge Carrico (Van Ness, Feldman and Curtis), Executive Director ◆ Bob Szabo (Van Ness, Feldman and Curtis), Counsel

Northern Community Advocates for Resource Equity (NORTHCARE)

Box 1405
North Bay, ON
P1B 8K6 Canada
also: North Road
Upsala, ON
P0T 2Y0 Canada
705 495 1199

N ORTHCARE, one of the first Canadian Share groups (see Chapter 2), was formed in 1987 by tourism, mining and timber companies and organizations. Headquartered in rugged northeast Ontario, NORTHCARE warns that a policy of "preservation" will undermine the entire economy of Ontario, and tells workers that environmental laws will destroy their livelihoods.

NORTHCARE attended the 1988 founding meeting of the Wise Use and Share movements in Reno, Nevada. Since then, its corporate sponsorship has grown to include transport companies, tourist outfitters, chambers of commerce, small businesses, trade associations and fur stores, as well as 69 timber towns and several school boards.

Funding (partial list of founding members)
Association of Tree Farmers of Ontario ♦ Elk Lake District Chamber of Commerce ♦ G.E.M.S. Tourist Camp Association ♦ Northern Prospectors Association ♦ Northeastern Ontario Chambers of Commerce ♦ Ontario Federation of Hunters and Anglers ♦ Ontario Trappers Association ♦ River Valley Tourist Operators Association ♦ Temagami Forest Products Association

Officers

Liz van Amelsfoort, President ♦ Dennis Price, Vice President ♦ Damaris Hansman, past President

Oregon Lands Coalition (OLC)

280 Court Street NE, #5
Salem OR 97301
503 363 8582

While the Oregon Lands Coalition claims to be a grassroots organization with 80,000 members in the Pacific Northwest, its 61 chapters consist of logging, mining and agricultural associations, and Wise Use anti-environmental groups. (The most prominent chapters are Associated Oregon Loggers, Oregonians for Food and Shelter, Oregon Farm Bureau Federation and the Oregon Cattlemen's Association.)

OLC coordinates statewide and national protests against the Endangered Species Act, pressures lawmakers to emasculate existing environmental legislation and mounts boycotts. In 1989, for instance, OLC led a boycott of Turner Broadcasting System for airing a "pro-preservation" National Audubon Society documentary called *Ancient Forests: Rage Over Trees.* Letter-writing, telephone and fax campaigns persuaded Ford, ITT-Rayonier, Hartford Insurance, Michelin Tire, Stroh's Brewery and several other firms to drop their sponsorship of the program, costing TBS $250,000 in lost revenue.

As OLC founder Valerie Johnson puts it, "environmentalists are really our hard-core enemies." In 1991, OLC used the controversy surrounding the spotted owl to raise most of its $145,000 budget. OLC helped draft the Community Stability Act of 1992, which would ban preservation of land that could otherwise be used for recreation or development. This law, which OLC says would "do for people what the Endangered Species Act does for animals," failed in 1992 but remains a priority on OLC's legislative agenda.

Funding (partial list)

American Forest Resource Council ♦ American Pulpwood Association ♦ Avison Lumber ♦ Boise Cascade ♦ Cascade Wood Products ♦ Fort Vancouver Lumber ♦ National Rifle Association ♦ Northwest Forestry Association ♦ Oregon Farm Bureau ♦ Puget Sound Trucking ♦ Seneca Sawmill ♦ Weyerhauser ♦ Zip-O-Log Mills

Officers

Valerie Johnson, President ♦ Judy Wortman, Secretary ♦ Charlie Janz, Chairman ♦ Evelyn Badger, Vice-Chairwoman ♦ Andy Anderson, Vice-Chairman ♦ Kevin Procter, Treasurer

Oregonians for Food and Shelter (OFS)

567 Union Street NE
Salem OR 97301
503 370 8092, 503 370 8565

Who can argue with an organization that supports the most basic of human needs—food and shelter? Who'd want people to go hungry or homeless? This group of Oregonians believes that's exactly what will happen if environmentalists succeed in restricting the use of certain chemicals that are sprayed on food and household pests. According to Oregonians for Food and Shelter, the public health and safety risk surrounding pesticide use is greatly exaggerated by environmentalists.

OFS organizes rural citizens by demonizing the environmental movement and latching onto heart-wrenching issues. Its newsletter claims that the Endangered Species Act is "a destroyer of jobs, families and communities" and that excessive pesticide regulation will result in "fewer jobs, fewer services, higher taxes and a substantial decrease in the quality of life as we know it today."

But even toxic chemicals that have been banned in the US are hazardous to manufacturing and transportation workers that must come in contact with them. And, according to the Food and Drug Administration, these exported poisons reappear on supermarket shelves in about 4.3% of imported foods.

Funding

The Board of Directors includes representatives from Boise Cascade ◆ Chevron Chemical ◆ DuPont ◆ Oregon Horticultural Society ◆ OR Ag Chemical and Fertilizer Association ◆ Western Agricultural Chemicals Association ◆ Pacific Northwest Aerial Applicators ◆ Weyerhauser

Officers

Dee Bridges, President ◆ Terry Witt, Executive Director ◆ Charles Henry, Secretary ◆ Paulette Pyle, Director of Grassroots ◆ Sandra Schukar, Office Manager

Pacific Legal Foundation (PLF)

2700 Gateway Oaks Dr, Suite 200
Sacramento CA 95833
916 641 8888
also: 121 West Fireweed Lane, Suite 250
Anchorage AK 99503
907 278 1731
also: 1200 One Union Square
Seattle WA 98101
206 389 7226

Founded in 1973, the Pacific Legal Foundation was the first of a new wave of right-wing "public-interest law firms" that actually represent the interests of big business. Its $4 million budget comes from chemical manufacturers, power companies, real estate developers, oil and timber companies and related foundations.

In the more than 100 lawsuits PLF has been involved in since 1990, it has challenged federal clean water regulations, tried to exempt industry from hazardous waste cleanup, moved to block wilderness designations and wetland protection, supported increased mining on public lands, and opposed corporate taxation. On virtually every issue, PLF comes down squarely in opposition to environmentalists.

Funding (partial list)

Alcoa Foundation ♦ American Farm Bureau Federation ♦ Amoco Foundation ♦ ARCO Foundation ♦ Lynde and Harry Bradley Foundation ♦ Chevron ♦ Coors Foundation ♦ Exxon Foundation ♦ Ford Motor Company Fund ♦ Georgia Pacific ♦ Gulf Oil Foundation ♦ William Randolph Hearst Foundation ♦

J.M. Foundation ♦ Eli Lilly Foundation ♦ Monsanto Fund ♦ M.J. Murdock Charitable Trust ♦ John M. Olin Foundation ♦ Pacific Gas and Electric ♦ Pacific Power and Light ♦ Phillips Petroleum ♦ Potlatch ♦ Rockwell International ♦ Sarah Scaife Foundation ♦ Texaco ♦ Union Carbide ♦ Weyerhauser Foundation

Officers

Robert F. Kane, Chairman ♦ Marc Sandstrom, Vice Chairman ♦ Douglas C. Jacobs, Secretary-Treasurer ♦ Ronald A. Zumbrum, President and CEO ♦ L. Shelton Olson, Executive Vice President

People for the West! (PFW!)

301 N Main
Pueblo CO 81003
719 543 8421

People for the West! claims to have organized more than a hundred chapters in ten states and involved them in a "grassroots" battle to safeguard "Western values." PFW! activists picket government buildings, testify at public hearings and confront environmentalists. Its projected budget for 1992 was $1.7 million.

PFW!'s chief crusade is a campaign to save the archaic 1872 Mining Law. Originally intended to encourage pick-axe prospectors by selling rights to mine on federal lands for a few dollars an acre, the law today is abused by large mining companies who buy claims for a fraction of their real market value. Not only are they using legal loopholes to exploit the environment, they're also depriving taxpayers of a fortune in lost revenues.

While many of PFW!'s individual members have no ties to the mining industry, the group is bankrolled by dozens of mining companies. Members are drawn in by PFW!'s propaganda, which blames society's ills on the environmental movement.

One foreboding PFW! pamphlet warns that if mining, grazing or logging are restricted, "people will lose jobs, rural communities will become ghost towns, education for our children will suffer and state and local governments will forfeit critical income for police, fire protection, roads and social services."

A Colorado rancher who founded a local PFW! chapter admitted, "I'm not real versed with the 1872 Mining Law, but it's worked real good for a lot of years. And [PFW! says] that if we don't protect our rights we could lose everything."

Funding (partial list)

Alaska Miners Corporation ♦ American Mining Congress ♦ Bond Gold ♦ Centurion Gold ♦ Chevron ♦ Cyprus Minerals ♦ Energy Fuels ♦ FMC Gold ♦ Hecla Mining ♦ Homestake Mining ♦ Minerex Resources ♦ Nerco Minerals ♦ Northwest Mining Congress ♦ Pegasus Mining ♦ US Precious Metals ♦ Western World Mining ♦ Westmont Mining

Officers

Thomas Albanese, Chairman and President ♦ Robert Reveles (Vice President, Homestake Mining), Vice Chair ♦ Pam Shouldis, Secretary/Treasurer ♦ John M. Wilson (President, Pegasus Gold), immediate Past Chairman ♦ Barbara Grannell, Executive Director

Political Economy Research Center (PERC)

502 South 19th Ave, Suite 211
Bozeman MT 59715
406 587 9591

The Political Economy Research Center is a think tank whose staff of academics, media flacks and associates churns out position papers and op-ed pieces with titles like *The Endangered Species Act: A Perverse Way to Protect Biodiversity* and *The Market—Conservation's Best Friend.* In *USA Today* and other newspapers, PERC blames environmentalism for creating a political crisis. PERC's Richard Stroup contends that before the growth of the green movement, "technology itself was cleansing the environment."

Under PERC's "free-market environmentalism (FME) alternative," market forces would fully regulate the rate of environmental preservation and destruction. Assure landowners of their constitutionally guaranteed "property rights," and PERC promises that they'll voluntarily protect their land in order to preserve its value.

"The free in FME refers to the individual liberty that only markets can provide," writes PERC's Terry Anderson, "and without that human freedom, environmental quality will be of little consequence."

Funding (partial list)
Amoco Foundation ♦ Carthage Foundation ♦ Lilly Endowment ♦ J.M. Foundation ♦ John M. Olin Foundation ♦ Sarah Scaife Foundation ♦ Burlington Northern ♦ Murdock Charitable Trust

Officers

Michael D. Copeland, Executive Director ♦ Terry L. Anderson, Senior Associate ♦ P.J. Hill, Senior Associate ♦ Jane S. Shaw, Senior Associate ♦ Richard L. Stroup, Senior Associate ♦ Donald L. Leal, Senior Research Associate ♦ Monica Lane Guenther, Treasurer

The President's Council on Competitiveness

Office of the Vice President
1600 Pennsylvania Ave NW
Washington DC 20036
202 456 6222

As anti-environmental organizations flourished during the Bush Administration, their strongest ally was Vice President Quayle, the chairman of the President's Council on Competitiveness. Bob Woodward of the *Washington Post* described the Council as "a command post for a war against government regulation of American business." This group of senior administration officials was authorized by President Bush to review, revise and even annul federal regulations.

Now disbanded, the Council rewrote key provisions of the Clean Air Act, weakened acid rain controls and narrowed the definition of wetlands. It also sabotaged attempts by the Environmental Protection Agency to ban incineration of lead batteries and to require 25% recycling of municipal waste—thus forcing EPA officials to violate established environmental law.

Secrecy and backroom-deal-making were hallmarks of Quayle's council. It resisted numerous Congressional attempts to investigate its role in undermining the Clean Air Act and its possible violations of the Ethics in Government Act. The Vice President himself was accused of conflict of interest by the Chairman of the House Subcommittee on Health and the Environment, Henry Waxman (D–CA).

"Specifically," Waxman wrote to his colleagues, "in December 1990, Mr. Quayle personally intervened to quash an EPA rulemaking [process] that would have triggered widespread recycling of newspapers." This, according to Waxman, benefitted Quayle's family trust, which controls newspapers in Indiana, invests in a virgin-paper mill and was, at the time, fighting mandatory newspaper recycling proposals.

Council director David McIntosh represented the Council at numerous gatherings of anti-environmental groups, including the 1992 Wise Use national leadership conference.

Funding

US taxpayers

Public Lands Council (PLC)

1301 Pennsylvania Ave NW, Suite 300
Washington DC 20004
202 347 5355, fax: 202 638 0607

The Public Lands Council was set up in 1968 by the National Cattlemen's Association, which represents about

360,000 cattle and sheep ranchers—everyone from large corporate agribusinesses to small family ranches. PLC lobbies Congress and government agencies for continued grazing rights on public lands.

The Bureau of Land Management (BLM) and US Forest Service together manage 270 million acres of rangeland in sixteen Western states. Environmentalists oppose overgrazing on these lands because it causes erosion and destroys wildlife habitat. According to 1989 BLM statistics, more than two-thirds of leased rangeland for which there was published data was in unsatisfactory condition.

Grazing on public land usually comes cheap. Fees are $1.92 per Animal Unit Month (AUM)—the amount of forage it takes to feed one cow for a month. Since the average private lease costs $7 per AUM, this amounts to granting enormous federal subsidies to ranchers using public lands. In fact, the fee is so low it doesn't even cover the cost of administering and maintaining the lands.

Only 2% of all cattle and sheep ranchers—mainly corporations and large individual ranchers—have grazing permits on federal lands. Small family ranchers are forced to lease private lands. In spite of this, PLC has won support from many of the other 98% of ranchers for give-away prices on grazing permits.

With branches in fourteen states, PLC is a member of the Alliance for America, the Environmental Conservation Organization and other Wise Use coalitions.

Funding

National Cattlemen's Association ♦ American Sheep Industry Association ♦ Association of National Grasslands

Officers

Pamela Neal, President ♦ Brian C. McDonald, Assistant Director

Putting People First (PPF)

4401 Connecticut Ave NW, Suite 310-A
Washington DC 20008
202 364 7277

Founder Kathleen Marquardt calls PPF a "grassroots consumer organization" that represents "the average American who drinks milk and eats meat, benefits from medical research, wears leather, wool and fur, hunts and fishes, owns a pet, goes to zoos, circuses and rodeos and who benefits from the wise and rational use of the earth's resources." She tells prospective funders that "PPF balances science, reason and common sense against the deception, coercion and terrorism of the environmental and animal-'rights' movement."

Marquardt is the rising star of the Wise Use movement. She started PPF, she says, after a representative of People for the Ethical Treatment of Animals (PETA) spoke at her daughter's suburban Washington elementary school. She calls PETA and other animal rights advocates "cultists" and extends that label to the environmental movement.

After receiving an award for best newcomer, she told a 1992 Wise Use leadership conference: "Here is our enemy—the Sierra Club, the Nature Conservancy, the Humane Society." Yes, that's right—according to PPF, the Humane Society is "a radical animal rights cult...a front for a neo-pagan cult that is attacking science, health and reason."

PPF is primarily a lobbying group for businesses that use animals for food, research, entertainment, recreation and clothing. "I do a lot for the poultry and egg people," Marquardt told the Washington Post.

After its first year of existence (1991–92), PPF boasted a membership of 35,000, with 100 chapters in 39 states and Canada, Europe, India and Africa. "We have a woman in Botswana who is very concerned about people getting killed by elephants," PPF spokesperson Mark LaRochelle said.

Marquardt's syndicated column, *Washington Report: From the Trenches*, is carried by *Fur Age Weekly*, *Poultry Times* and *Soldier of Fortune*. In it, Marquardt has accused Greenpeace of having "terrorist connections" and of working with the KGB.

PPF and Marquardt have organized corporate boycotts, circulated Congressional petitions and formed a Political Action Committee (PPF-PAC) that's authorized to endorse political candidates and engage in partisan political work. In 1992, PPF-PAC ranked all 535 members of Congress for their voting records on resource management, conservation and property rights, and then mobilized voters on behalf of those who fared well. The "stars" of this survey were Don Young (R–AK) and Charles Stenholm (D–TX). Among the "worst," according to PPF-PAC, were Barbara Boxer (D–CA), Ron Dellums (D–CA) and Pat Schroeder (D–CO).

Funding

PPF doesn't publicly disclose its members, and claims to be supported only by membership dues. About 50 hunting clubs, trapping associations, kennels, furriers, circuses, carriage horse companies and rodeos—the PPF Association Network—are the largest donors.

Officers

Kathleen Marquardt, Executive Director ♦ Mark LaRochelle, Media Director ♦ Bill Wewer, Legal Counsel

The Reason Foundation (RF)

3415 Sepulveda Blvd
Los Angeles CA 90034
310 391 2245, fax: 310 391 4395

The Reason Foundation is the largest right-wing think tank outside of Washington. Its philosophy is summed up by its motto, *free minds and free markets*, and it calls environmentalism "the most potent force for reregulation of the economy."

RF President Robert W. Poole believes the free market is a more effective tool than government regulation for environmental protection. "Free market-based principles," he says, "have led to waste reductions and demonstrated the counter-productive effects of many proposed [regulatory] mandates."

Poole's corporate supporters tend to agree. Oil and coal companies, investment firms, chemical manufacturers and a dozen right-wing charities contributed over $1 million to RF in 1991. Another million was raised in individual contributions and through selling books, white papers and other publications.

RF's primary educational and lobbying tool is *Reason* magazine (circulation, 40,000). Consumer Alert and C-FACT have invited RF to join their boards of directors, and tapped it for speakers.

Mainstream media is also becoming a forum for RF's anti-regulatory, anti-environmentalist views. The *New York Times, Washington Post, Los Angeles Times, Wall Street Journal,* ABC, NBC, CBS, CNN and dozens of radio stations all turned to the Reason Foundation for news, opinion and commentary in 1991 and 1992.

Funding (partial list)

American Farm Bureau Federation ♦ Ameritech ♦ Amoco Foundation ♦ Anheuser-Busch ♦ ARCO Foundation ♦ Bechtel International ♦ Lynde & Harry Bradley Foundation ♦ Chevron ♦ Coca-Cola Foods ♦ Coors ♦ Eli Lilly ♦ Exxon ♦ Ford Motor Company Fund ♦ General Dynamics ♦ J.M. Foundation ♦ Koch Charitable Foundation ♦ Liberty Fund ♦ Lilly Endowment ♦ Philip M. McKenna Foundation ♦ John M. Olin Foundation ♦ Mobil ♦ Perot Group ♦ Pfizer ♦ Philip Morris ♦ Phillips Petroleum ♦ Sarah Scaife Foundation ♦ Smith Richardson Foundation ♦ Texaco ♦ Xerox Foundation

Officers

Robert W. Poole, Jr., President ♦ Bryan Snyder, Senior Vice President ♦ Virginia I. Postrell, Editor, Reason ♦ Lynn Scarlett, Vice President, Research

Sahara Club USA

17939 Chatsworth St, Suite 525
Granada Hills CA 91344
818 368 4304, electronic bulletin board: 818 893 1899

Rick Siemen founded the Sahara Club in 1990 to attack environmentalists, who he blames for the closing of trails and roads that once were open to dirt-bikers. "Declare something endangered and forget about hard-earned freedom and rights," Siemen says.

Named to thumb its nose at the Sierra Club, the Sahara Club expresses its views in blunt, vulgar language. It calls Greenpeace "a bunch of lying, evil, cretinous, scum-sucking, larcenous, vile, money-grubbing bastards." Siemen explains: "Yes, we're rude, crude and obnoxious at times. [It's] like tossing cold water on a pair of fighting dogs. It's shocking, but it gets the job done."

But the Sahara Club goes beyond calling names—it also encourages physical violence against environmental activists. It publishes their names, addresses and even vehicle license numbers and says, "Now you know who they are and where they are. Just do the right thing and let your conscience be your guide." Siemen has given "dirty tricks" workshops, in which he shares Sahara's intimidation tactics with Mothers' Watch and other anti-environmental groups.

A special division of the Sahara Club known as the Clubbers—"big, tall, ugly desert riders," wielding baseball bats and "bad attitudes"— was created to deter environmentalists from staging public protests. During the "Redwood Summer" in California in 1990, Sahara Club offered a $100 bounty for the apprehension and arrest of environmental protesters. No bounties were paid, but many environmentalists were physically assaulted. The following spring, a Sahara Club member was arrested for placing a fake bomb in the offices of the Arcata Action Center, an environmental organization.

Funding (partial list of financial or in-kind supporters)

Midwest Action Cycles ♦ JT Racing ♦ O'Neal ♦ AXO Sport ♦ Pro-Circuit ♦ Sun Line ♦ Gold Belt ♦ Scotts ♦ Thor Racing ♦ Superlift ♦ Pro-Tec ♦ Works Performance ♦ The Desert Vipers Motorcycle Club ♦ Conejo Trail Riders ♦ Moose Racing ♦ Sunland Shamrocks Motorcycle Club

Officers

Rick Sieman, President ♦ Louis McKey, Vice President ♦ Arlene Valdez, Newsletter Graphics/Art Director ♦ Corrinne Jensen, Office Manager/Secretary ♦ Pat Martin, Electronic Surveillance/Sysop ♦ Rocky Nunzio, Security

Science and Environmental Policy Project (SEPP)

2101 Wilson Boulevard, Suite 1003
Arlington VA 22201
703 527 0131, fax: 703 276 2673

Science and Environmental Policy Project was founded in 1990 as an affiliate of the Washington Institute for Values in Public Policy, a Moonie-funded think tank. Its stated purpose is to "document the relationship between scientific data and the development of federal environmental policy." Its goal is to discredit global warming, ozone depletion and acid rain as a fantasy of politically-motivated environmentalists.

Director Fred Singer's views on these issues have made him a popular scientific panelist at anti-environmental conferences, and a leading critic of the environmental movement. "We are disturbed that activists, anxious to stop energy and economic growth, are pushing ahead with drastic policies without taking notice of recent changes in the underlying science," wrote Singer in a statement circulated to colleagues.

Singer places the blame for the world's social crises squarely on the environmental movement. He claims that global warming is most likely a harmless natural occurrence, that the burning of fossil fuel increases the world's food supply and that global regulations will "have catastrophic impacts on the world economy, on jobs, standards of living and health care."

In an attempt to undermine the 1992 Earth Summit treaty on global warming, SEPP distorted the results of a Greenpeace survey of atmospheric scientists, to try to suggest that there's no consensus that CO_2 emissions pose a serious environmental threat. According to SEPP, the Greenpeace poll showed that "any future climate warming is likely to be minor, and even benign to human existence on the planet."

In fact, 45% of the 113 scientists who responded to the Greenpeace survey believe that the earth is reaching a point of no return, where global warming will become uncontrollable and irreversible. And all the scientists responding agree that global warming is a problem, caused in large part by the emission of greenhouse gases produced by man-made industries and autos.

Funding
Bradley Foundation ♦ Smith-Richardson Foundation ♦ Forbes Foundation

Officers
Dr. S. Fred Singer, Executive Director ♦ Candace Crandall, Editorial Director

Scientists and Engineers for Secure Energy (SE²)

570 Seventh Av., Suite 1007
New York NY 100018
212 840 6595

Scientists and Engineers for Secure Energy is a scientific think tank funded by the nuclear energy lobby. It claims to have 200 "professional" members and lists 42 scientists on its letterhead, including six Nobel Prize winners in physics and chemistry.

SE^2 was founded in the mid-1970's to persuade the public that nuclear energy is a safe and efficient alternative energy source. Today, SE^2 experts promise that global warming, acid rain and ozone depletion can be averted by a switch to nuclear technology.

Chairman Frederick Seitz discounts alternatives like solar and geothermal power (combined with energy efficiency) as too "expensive" and "unrealistic." The solution to this crisis, according to Seitz, is to build new nuclear power plants and prohibit public hearings in which local citizens can give input.

Funding

US Council for Energy Awareness ♦ SE^2 conferences throughout the 1980s were co-sponsored by numerous trade associations and public utilities, including: American Nuclear Society ♦ American Institute of Chemical Engineers ♦ American Association of Electrical Engineers ♦ Pacific Gas and Electric

Officers

Frederick Seitz, Chairman ♦ Erich Isaac, Vice Chairman ♦ Robert K. Adair, Vice Chairman ♦ Joseph B. Scrandris, Comptroller ♦ Miro M. Todorovich, Executive Director ♦ Millicent J. Scrandris, Assistant to the Executive Director

The Sea Lion Defense Fund (SLDF)

Box 2296
Kodiak AK 99618
907 486 3234, 907 486 3033

Sea lions once thrived along the southwestern Alaska coast, but their numbers decreased by over 50% between 1960 and 1985, and another 5% between 1991 and 1992. They're disappearing so rapidly that they've been declared a threatened species.

Despite its name, the Sea Lion Defense Fund is no friend to this creature. It's the legal arm of Alaska's fishing industry, founded in 1991 in response to a lawsuit that was filed after the National Marine Fisheries Service increased the fishing quota on pollock, the seals' main food, by 40%.

Fearing this huge increase would decimate both the pollock stocks and the seals, and forever alter the marine ecosystem in the Gulf of Alaska, Greenpeace and the Sierra Club Legal Defense Fund sued the Fisheries Service for violation of the Endangered Species Act, the Magnuson Fishery Conservation and Management Act and the National Environmental Policy Act.

The fishing industry and its local dependents took a different view. Hailing the new quota as a boon, they set up the SLDF to fight the environmentalists' suit. Their intervention was successful, and the new quotas went into effect. Greenpeace and the SLDF continue to litigate over future quotas.

Funding

Municipalities, fishing vessels, fish processors, fishing trade associations, local businesses, shipyards, packing and equipment suppliers.

Officers

Ken Allread, Western Alaska Fisheries ♦ Al Burch, Alaska Draggers Association ♦ Gary Bloomquist, City of Kodiak ♦ Jerome Selby, Kodiak Island Borough

Share B.C.

Box 1074
Ucluelet BC
V0R 3A0 Canada
604 726 2002, fax: 604 726 1254

Share B.C., also known as the Citizens Coalition for Sustainable Development, is a coalition of citizen groups opposed to "forest preservation." Made up of Share our Forests, Share the Stein, Share the Rock, Share our Resources, Share the Clayoquot and twenty other organizations, it claims a combined membership of 24,000.

Share B.C. provides its member groups, many of which are in isolated rural areas, with media contacts and networking possibilities, both in Canada and overseas. Share B.C. was even accredited by the U.N. as a nongovernmental organization for the Rio Earth Summit.

Share B.C.'s main agenda is to keep public and private old-growth forest available for logging. According to Robert E. Skelly, who represents Port Alberni, B.C. in the House of Commons, Share B.C. was set up in 1988 by Bob Findlay, who is currently CEO of the timber-industry giant MacMillan Bloedel.

Skelly attended the founding meeting, along with Jack Toovey, Fletcher Challenge's former vice president for forestry, and Patrick Armstrong, one of B.C.'s leading anti-environmentalists. Soon after, MacMillan Bloedel executives suggested to its employees that they also set up Share groups, and offered them financial assistance to do so.

Each Share group focusses on a local preservation effort. Share the Cloyquot, set up to prevent expansion of the Pacific Rim National Park, tells the public that clearcuts are "one step in the renewable resource cycle." Share Our Forests sponsored a contest in Vancouver Island schools, offering a $3,000 prize for the best student essay on the theme "why clearcut logging is beneficial for B.C."

Share B.C. offers free timber tours, given by clear-cutters like Fletcher Challenge and MacMillan Bloedel. Moving from logging site to mill, these tours present the idea that trees can be regenerated or regrown in just a few years. The Canadian timber industry, however, cuts old-growth forests almost exclusively, and they take over 200 years to regenerate.

Funding

Share B.C. admitted that 60% of its 1991 operating costs were paid for by forest corporations. However, as with all Share groups, the identity of these corporate funders is kept secret.

Officers

John Bassingthwaite, immediate Past Chairman ♦ Danny Taylor, Interim Chairman ♦ Bill Beldessi, Chairman ♦ Michael Morton, Executive Director

Society for Environmental Truth (SET)

625 N Van Buren, Suite 216
Tucson AZ 85711
602 790 4769

The Society for Environmental Truth was founded in 1992 by R.S. Bennet, a retired forestry teacher who believes that environmental policy is driven by "irrational thought." He envisions a broad grassroots movement that would debunk the views of "eco-terrorists" like Greenpeace. SET organizes protests, arranges legislative testimonies and uses the media to disseminate the results of industry-backed studies. Its motto is, *get SET for the truth.*

According to SET, endangered species, global warming and ozone depletion are bogus issues, created by environmentalists solely to pad their already bulging bank accounts. "For the past several years," says Bennett, "the major environmental organizations have resorted to lies, half-truths and unsubstantiated theories to prod generous Americans to donate to their causes."

SET Secretary H.R. Jernigan compares the environmental movement's success to the rise of German fascism during the 1930s. "The Nazis had the Jews for a scapegoat, these [environmental] groups have big business. The Nazis had their own newspaper, the local groups have theirs. These groups are far more subtle than the Nazis, but their goal is the same: gain control of the government."

Funding

SET is funded by its membership, which is currently limited to local businesses and individual members.

Officers

R.S. Bennet, Executive Director ♦ H.R. Jernigan, Secretary

US Council for Energy Awareness (USCEA)

1776 I St NW, Suite 400
Washington DC 20006
202 293 0770

The US Council for Energy Awareness is the official public-relations branch of the nuclear power industry. It was established in 1980 in response to widespread public mistrust and fear after the disaster at the Three Mile Island nuclear power plant. Nearly 400 power companies in the US and abroad chip in to supply USCEA's $20 million+ annual budget.

USCEA's campaigns try to convince the public that nuclear power reduces dependence on foreign oil, stimulates economic growth and, because it produces no greenhouse gases, is ecologically sound. But the public isn't buying, and the US nuclear power industry remains in crisis. No new reactors have been ordered since 1973, and reactors now operating are shutting prematurely.

Despite billions of tax dollars spent on research, there's still no safe way to dispose of the tons of radioactive waste power plants produce, which can remain toxic for up to 220,000 years. Even the *Wall Street Journal* points out that all nuclear plants completed between 1980 and 1988 had cost overruns ranging from 200% to 2400%!

Needless to say, the USCEA paints a totally different picture. A newspaper ad showing a newly hatched baby turtle scooting across a stretch of beach touts the scene as "more evidence of the truth of nuclear energy: it peacefully coexists with the environment."

A TV spot shows an attractive, personable, intelligent woman explaining her concerns about the environment and her recent change of heart: "I want my kids to grow up in a healthy environment....When I was in college, I was against nuclear energy. But I've reached a different conclusion. It means cleaner air for the planet."

Documents leaked to Greenpeace reveal that these ads were part of a strategy targeting women during 1992, the "Year of the Woman." According to a USCEA-commissioned survey, "public opinion polls show that American women are less well-informed about nuclear energy than men....[but that] with increased awareness, women's support can increase." The USCEA found that after telling women that "nuclear energy cuts greenhouse gas emissions and air pollution," their attitudes towards nukes were measurably softened.

Funders (partial list)

American Electric Power Service Corp ◆ American Nuclear Corp ◆ Atomic Energy of Canada ◆ Bechtel Power Corp ◆ Chem Nuclear Systems ◆ Commonwealth Edison ◆ Department of Energy, Mines and Resources of Canada ◆ Dresser Industries ◆ Energy Resources International ◆ Exxon ◆ General Electric ◆ Martin Marietta Energy Systems ◆ Union Pacific ◆ Uranium Resources ◆ Westinghouse

Officers

Phillip Bayne, President and CEO ◆ Bill Harris, Senior Vice President ◆ Carl A. Goldstein, Vice President, Public and Media Relations ◆ Edward L. Aduss, Vice President, Advertising ◆ Richard J. Meyers, Vice President, Industry Communications and Publications ◆ Marvin S. Fertel, Vice President, Technical Programs ◆ Ann S. Bisconti, Vice President, Research and Program Evaluation

Wilderness Impact Research Foundation (WIRF)

555 6th St
Elko NV 89801
702 738 2009

The Wilderness Impact Research Foundation is a national organization formed in 1986 to fight new Wilderness Area designations proposed under the

federal Wilderness Act. In seminars, conferences, media appearances and lobbying,
WIRF publicizes the "negative impact" that
wilderness area protection has on mining,
skiing, hunting and ranching.

Founder A. Grant Gerber is one of the principal leaders of the Wise Use, or as he prefers
to call it, Multiple Use, movement. "Our focus
is factual," says Gerber, "what is best for the
people, the wildlife, the land." Yet he calls
environmentalists "pantheists" (those who
believe that God is present in everything) and
"druids" (members of an ancient, nature-wor-
shipping Celtic religion).

Two key pieces of environmental legislation,
the Wilderness Preservation System and the
Endangered Species Act, are the chief targets
of WIRF's attacks. Each year WIRF, together
with the Mountain States and Pacific Legal
Foundations, organizes National Wilderness
Conferences to lure members to their anti-
environmentalist cause.

Attendees include hundreds of representatives of the timber, oil, cattle, mining and
recreation industries. Participants in 1991
included the American Forest Council, the
American Petroleum Institute, the National
Cattleman's Association, the American Mining Congress, the National Rifle Association,
as well as a number of other groups listed in
this book.

Funding

WIRF's National Steering Committee includes
Rocky Mountain Oil and Gas Association ◆ National
Forest Products Association ◆ National Cattlemen's

Association ♦ American Motorcyclist Association ♦ Northwest Mining Association

Officers

A. Grant Gerber, Executive Director and Treasurer ♦ Thomas Porter, President ♦ Mark O. Walsh, Secretary

Yellow Ribbon Coalition (YRC)

655 North A St
Springfield OR 97477
503 747 5874, fax: 503 747 0612

The Yellow Ribbon Coalition is a Wise Use lobby for the timber industry, with branches in Oregon, Washington and California. Although it claims to be a grassroots organization representing thousands of unemployed or "at-risk" workers and their families, YRC is directed by company executives. Its motto is, *saving jobs and supporting communities.*

The YRC says it speaks on behalf of "those who cannot [put] their thoughts and feelings into fancy words that others would understand." It's designed public school curricula that it claims have reached 10,000 students, and has lobbied state assemblies and federal agencies throughout the country.

Individuals, families and businesses can become members. Special provisions are made for Yellow Ribbon Workplaces—companies where employees donate via payroll deduction. These companies are included on YRC's board of directors.

YRC is known for organizing high-profile protests and counter protests that blame environmentalists for the rising unemployment rate. "Mills are closing. Hard working men and women—family people—are losing their jobs, the direct result of preservationists' lawsuits [and] fraudulent claims," reads a typical YRC ad in a timber trade magazine. YRC has gained national visibility through its membership in two Wise Use coalitions—the Oregon Lands Coalition and the Alliance for America.

Funding

In 1992–93, the board represented Triangle Veneer ♦ Tom Borland ♦ Eugene Chamber ♦ Seneca Sawmill ♦ Zip-O-Log Mills ♦ Centennial Bank ♦ Heath Logging ♦ Swanson Brothers ♦ TECO ♦ Starfire Lumber ♦ JMC Logging & Farming ♦ Lane Plywood ♦ Emerald Forest Products ♦ Diamond Wood Products ♦ Rexius Forest Products

Officers

Jim Welsh, President ♦ Bonnie Morgan, Internal Vice President ♦ Mike McKay, External Vice President ♦ Suzanne Penegor, Secretary ♦ Konrad Lohner, Treasurer ♦ Charlie Janz, Past President

Notes

Sources for the facts and quotations in this book are listed below by page numbers and brief subject descriptions. Full publication data is given the first time a work is cited.

7.   Ex-forestry official quote. Bill Holmes (speech reprint) "Weirdos Wimps and Watermelons," *Anderson Valley Advertiser,* 4/24/91.

8.   Projected sales of "green" products. Winski, Joseph M. "Green Marketing: Big Prizes but No Easy Answers," *Advertising Age,* 10/28/91.

8.   Export of wood products. *Forest Watch,* Cascade Economic Holistic Consultants, Jul 91, Vol 12, No. 1, pp. 26–27.

9.   Mobil Chemical quote. Greenpeace Plastics Fact Sheet, 1990.

9.   Mobil sued. Reuters, 7/28/92. Schneider, Keith, "Guides on Environmental Ad Claims," *New York Times,* 7/29/92.

10. EPA lawsuit. "E Notes," *E Magazine,* May/Jun 92.

12. Violent attacks against environmentalists. Franklin, Jonathan, "First They Kill your Dog," *Muckraker,* Jan 93.

13. Bush quote. Medford, Oregon speech, 9/14/92. Transcript.

14. Conservative court bias. "The Federal Courts at a Crossroads" Alliance for Justice Judicial Selection Project, *Annual Report,* Washington DC, 1992.

17–18. Tulane study. Houck, Oliver. "With Charity For All," *Yale Law Journal,* Jul 84.

18. Money from charities in 1991. *1992 Grantmakers' Guide,* The Foundation Center, Washington DC, 1992.

19. "Exploit the environment for private gain." Long, Katherine, "A Grinch Who Loathes Green Groups," *The Toronto Star,* 12/21/91; Udall, Stewart L. and Kent Olsen, "Me First and Nature Second," *Los Angeles Times,* 7/27/92.

19. "Do things industry can't." Latter, Carol & Juanita Haddad, "Sharing with the Share Groups," *The Leaflet,* Pulp, Paper & Woodworkers of Canada, Jan 89.

19–20. AFC and Moon cult. Anderson, Scott and John Lee Anderson, *Inside the League,* Dodd, Mead & Co., New York, 1986, pp. 64–65; Report on the Share Phenomenon, Executive Summary, Parliamentary Library, House of Commons, Ottowa, May 92.

20–21. Wise Use goals. Gottlieb Alan, ed. *The Wise Use Agenda,* The Free Enterprise Press, Bellevue, Washington, 1989.

21. Parliamentary Library report. Report on the Share Phenomenon.

24. AIM linked to Rev. Moon. Wolf, Louis, "Accuracy in Media Rewrites the News and History," *Covert Action Information Bulletin,* Number 21, p. 36.

25. Environment in the media. "FAIR Study: Amount of Environmental Coverage Slips in 1991," *EXTRA!,* Apr/May, 92.

25. AIM funding. 1992 *Grantmakers Guide;* Wolf, *Covert Action Information Bulletin,* pp. 26–28, 36.

26. Oil in ANWR. Greenpeace Arctic Fact Sheet. 1991.

29. AER harassment of environmentalists. Ball, Gary "Wise Use Nuts and Bolts," *Mendocino Environmental Center Newsletter,* Issue 12, Summer/Fall 92; Judi Bari, phone interview with author, Oct 92.

31. Hartmann, Carolyn and Bill Walsh, Dupont Fiddles While the World Burns, USPIRG report, 12/11/89.

32. Pak quote. "Moonies Are More Active and Gaining Influence," *Group Research Report,* Summer 89, p. 1.

33. Sikorsky, Merrill, "In Search of an Energy Policy for America," *American Freedom Journal,* Oct 90.

33. "five years of oil." Greenpeace Arctic Fact sheet, 1991.

33. AFC funding. Seltzer, Andrew, "Grassroots Movement to Exploit Federal Wilderness Organized by Moonie Front," *Portland Free Press,* 11/16/89.

37. Margaret Durante, Burson-Marstellar (New York), phone interview with author, Nov 92.

38. CDC a front for mining companies, etc. "Desert Coalition Descends on Washington," *BlueRibbon,* Jul 91, p. 14; AP "Groups that Use Desert Are Opposed to Preservation," *Sacramento Bee,* 4/7/91, p. B15.

39. "Relieve people of property." *Desert News Letter,* quoting Wayne Hage, Jun 92, p. 2.

40. Simon quote "gloom and doom." "Apocalypse in Rio: The End of the World As We Know It?" *CATO Policy Report,* Jul/Aug, 92, pp. 6–7.

40. Taylor, Jerry, "Beware of Eco-treaties," *USA Today,* 5/29/92.

40. Funding. CATO Institute *Annual Report,* 1991.

41. Arnold quote. Long, Katherine, *Portland Oregonian,* 12/16/91.

41. Destroy free enterprise. Long, Katherine, "A Grinch Who Loathes Green Groups," *The Toronto Star,* 12/21/91.

41–42. $5 million annually. Egan, Timothy "125 Groups Put their Anti-Environmental Eggs in One Basket," New York Times News Service, 1/1/92.

42. CDFE funding. Gottlieb, *The Wise Use Agenda,* pp. 157–66.

44. Gold quote. Speech before US EPA National Environmental Information Conference, Philadelphia, 12/4/91.

44. CFE funding. Citizens for a Sound Economy, *Annual Report*, 1991.

48. "Ruthless predecessors." *Citizen Outlook,* May/Jun 92.

49. CA positions. Magelli, Mark and Andy Friedman. *Masks of Deception,* Essential Information, Washington DC, 1991, p. 80.

49–50. Greenhouse effect. "Global Warning—The Myth," *Consumer Comments,* Vol. 14, No. 5, Sep 90.

50–51. Roger Marzulla. *National Journal,* Update section, 3/7/92.

54. FREE's budget growth. IRS 990 form, 1990.

55. Total privatization. Baden, John, "Oil and Ecology Do Mix," *The Wall Street Journal,* 2/24/87.

56. Miller quote. Lippmann, Thomas, "Energy Lobby Fights Unseen 'Killers,'" *Washington Post,* 4/1/92, p. A21.

56. GCC's role at the Earth Summit. Bruno, Kenny, "The Corporate Capture of the Earth Summit," *Multinational Monitor,* Jul/Aug 1992, p. 15.

57. Heritage Foundation budget. Heritage Foundation *Annual Report,* 1991.

58. Policy blueprint. Andrews, John K., et al., "The Vision Thing: Conservatives Take Aim at the 90's," *Policy Review,* Spring 90, p. 4.

58. Meyerson, Adam. "The Vision Thing, Continued: A Conservative Research Agenda for the 90's," *Policy Review,* Summer 90, p. 2.

60. "Precipitous legislation." "Why is Minneapolis Getting Colder?" ICE information packet, Nov 92.

60. Directing advertising. O'Driscoll, Mary, *The Energy Daily,* 6/24/91, p. 1.

61. "Future challenges." *Liberty & Law,* Fall 92.

62. US landfills. *50 Simple Things You Can Do to Save The Earth,* Berkeley, CA, The Earth Works Group, Earthworks Press, 1989, p. 66.

63. Powers quote, Williams, Ted, "The Metamorphosis of Keep America Beautiful," *Audubon,* Mar 90.

63. Bottle-bill opposition. Magelli, *Masks of Deception,* p. 118.

63. Composting. Magelli, *Masks of Deception,* p. 117.

64. Pendley quote. Personal interview, Washington DC, 9/16/92.

64. Collusion. Bellant, Russ. *The Coors Connection,* South End Press, 1991, pp. 87–90.

64–65. MLSF reputation. Bellant, p. 80, quoting the *Rocky Mountain News,* 1981.

65. MLSF funding. *The Foundation Grants Index,* 1992.

69. Therberg quote. Houck, *Yale Law Journal,* p. 1475.

70. NLCPI fuunding. *The Foundation Grants Index,* 1992; Houck, *Yale Law Journal,* pp. 1474-76.

70. Wetlands revenue. Magelli, *Masks of Deception,* p. 140.

74. 1991 budget. Durbin, Kathie, *Portland Oregonian,* 1/27/92, p. B1.

76. PLF cases. Pacific Legal Foundation, *Annual Report,* 1992.

76–77. PLF funding. *The Foundation Grants Index,* 1992; Magelli, *Masks of Deception,* p. 155.

78. Rancher quote. *High Country News,* 7/1/91.

79. Stroup, Richard L. and Jane S. Shaw, *The Public Interest,* Fall 89.

79. Anderson, Terry and Donald Leal, "Free Market Environmentalism," *Econ Update,* May 92.

79. PERC funding. *The Foundation Grants Index,* 1992.

84. Marquardt quote. McCombs, Phil, "Attack of the Omnivore," *Washington Post,* 3/27/92, p. B4.

84. "Our enemy."CBS News 60 Minutes, transcript, Vol. XXV No. 2, 9/20/92, Livingston, NJ: Burrelle's Information Services, p. 16.

84. Humane Society. "The People's Agenda," Jan 92.

84. Greenpeace accusation. Marquardt, Kathleen. "Greenpeace On Earth, Bad Will Toward Man," *Soldier of Fortune,* Mar 92, p. 36.

86. Reason Foundation funding. Reason Foundation *Annual Report,* 1991.

87. "Job done." Sieman, Rick, Editorial, *Sahara Club, USA Newsletter,* #7, p. 1.

87. "Scum-sucking, etc." *Sahara Club, USA Newsletter,* #16.

87. Workshops. *Sahara Club, USA Newsletter,* #9.

91. Seitz, Frederick, "Must We Have Nuclear Power?" *Reader's Digest,* Aug 90.

92. Sea lion numbers. Merrick, Richard, D.G. Calkins and C. McAllister, *Aerial and Ship-based Surveys of Stellar Sea Lions (Eumatopias Jubatus) in SE Alaska, the Gulf of Alaska and the Aleutian Islands during June and July 1991.* National Oceanic Administration Technical Memorandum, National Marine Fisheries Service, 1992, Alaska Fisheries Science Center–1.

94. Share B.C.'s founding meeting. Letter from Robert Skelly, M.P. to Ron Neil, Fletcher Challenge, 4/28/92.

99. "Pantheists, druids." Knox, Margaret, "The Wise Use Guys," *Buzzworm,* Vol. 11, No. 6, Nov/Dec 90.

Index

More books in the Real Story series
(see the next page for other titles)

Who Killed Martin Luther King?
Philip Melanson

This fascinating investigation of a murder that changed history shows why the official story just doesn't make sense. *Spring, 1993*

Who Killed Robert Kennedy?
Philip Melanson

This provocative book explores numerous loopholes in the official explanation of the RFK assassination, and points to possible culprits.

Spring, 1993

Who Killed JFK?   Carl Oglesby

This brief but fact-filled book gives you the inside story on the most famous crime of this century. You won't be able to put it down.

Spring, 1992

Real Story books are available at most good bookstores, or send $5 per book + $2 shipping *per order* (not per book) to Odonian Press, Box 7776, Berkeley CA 94707. Please write for information on quantity discounts, or call us at 800 REAL STORY or 510 524 4000.